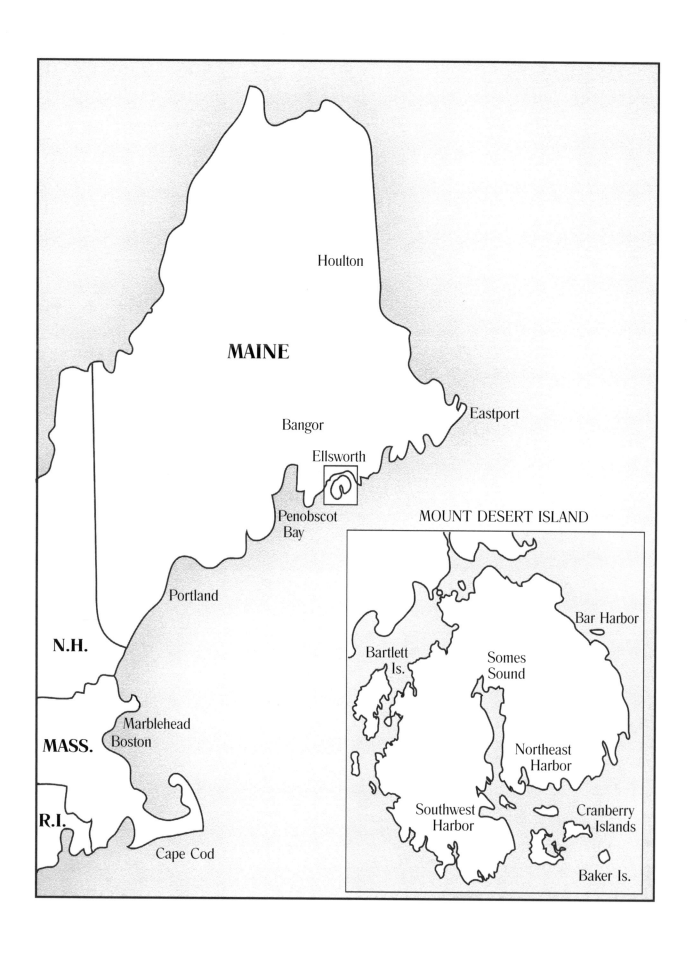

Houlton

MAINE

Bangor

Eastport

Ellsworth

Penobscot
Bay

MOUNT DESERT ISLAND

Portland

N.H.

Bartlett
Is.

Somes
Sound

Bar Harbor

Marblehead
Boston

MASS.

Northeast
Harbor

R.I.

Southwest
Harbor

Cranberry
Islands

Cape Cod

Baker Is.

RALPH STANLEY

Tales of a Maine Boatbuilder

By

CRAIG S. MILNER AND

RALPH W. STANLEY

Down East Books

Down East Books
P.O. Box 679
Camden, ME 04843
A division of Down East Enterprise, publishers of Down East *magazine,* www.downeast.com

To request a book catalog or place an order, visit www.downeastbooks.com, or call 800-685-7962.

To my wife, Evelyn, who inspired me.
C.M.

To my collaborator, Craig Milner; my wife, Marion; my children, Nadine,
Marjorie, Richard, and Edward; and all the relatives, friends, neighbors, and
teachers who supported and helped me along the way.
R.S.

Table of Contents

Introduction

In the mid-1970s, I was a young reporter and photographer working for a weekly newspaper in down east Maine. One of my responsibilities was to write feature articles, and I traveled around Hancock County looking for colorful characters to interview.

The coast of Maine was a rich source for my stories, and I particularly enjoyed the people and the activity I found in the boatyards. At that time quite a few small shops on Mount Desert Island were building traditional wooden boats just as they had for years. These craftsmen were older, and their work and their stories were fascinating.

There was also a new group of entrepreneurs who were making workboats and pleasure boats in fiberglass. Both could be produced much more quickly using this technology, and it came to dominate the boatbuilding industry in Maine. It appeared that wooden-boat construction was becoming a thing of the past in the state.

So when I heard that a builder named Ralph Stanley was about to start work on a new wooden boat, I though it would be a great opportunity to document the traditional construction process from the ground up. I went to his shop in Southwest Harbor and found him ready to begin a new Friendship sloop called *Freedom*. He was already rebuilding an original Friendship called *Morning Star*. I asked if I could take pictures as the work progressed, and he said, "Okay."

For nearly two years, I visited Ralph's shop weekly to photograph the various stages of construction. It was interesting to watch the boats evolve from pieces of wood to finished vessels ready to launch and sail, and I felt lucky to be allowed into this private world that few people ever see.

From the first time I watched one of Ralph's hulls taking shape, I realized that there was much more going on here than just craftsmanship. He takes the design and building of a utilitarian object—a boat—and elevates it to the level of sculpture. Whether it's a Friendship sloop, a lobster boat, or a vessel of a different design, each is a unique expression of his personal vision and creativity.

From a historical perspective, Ralph Stanley is a pivotal figure in traditional boatbuilding. He stands as a vital link in the unbroken chain of builders of the past, having learned his trade when *all* boat construction involved wood and men who had worked with this material all their lives, as had generations before them.

At the same time, Ralph represents a bridge to the future, not just maintaining tradition but advancing it. By his example, he has given inspiration and direction to others. By continuing to develop his methods of working with wood, he had extended the options and vocabulary for contemporary builders. And by his willingness to share and teach, he has passed on this knowledge to a new generation that is committed to wooden boats. Ralph's legacy also continues through his son Edward, who is a naval architect and marine engineer, and through his son Richard, who is a fine boatbuilder in his own right.

When I began, my idea was to write a book about how Friendship sloops are built, and the interviews I did with Ralph in the 1970s focused mostly on the history and construction of these graceful boats. That project never came together as expected, but the photos did provide the basis for a slide presentation to the Friendship Sloop Society, illustrations for an article in an international boating publication, and a number of photographic exhibits in Boston and Maine.

Over the years, I kept in touch with Ralph and would drop by the shop from time to time to visit him and see what was going on. Then, in the fall of 1998, I talked with him once again about the possibility of doing a book, and we began a new series of interviews. Through our discussions, I gained an even greater appreciation for his sense of humor and his delight in story-telling.

My hope for this book is that it will help readers get to know Ralph Stanley as I have, through the tales he tells of the people and experiences that have shaped him. After nearly thirty years, I continue to admire his humanity, dedication, and commitment. But what still impresses me most about Ralph is his artistry. The boats he has built are at once practical and elegant, and they represent an outstanding body of beautiful work.

Ralph has received a number of accolades for his contributions to boatbuilding and to the traditional arts and cultural heritage of Maine and the nation. He has been chosen as a National Heritage Fellow and has been named the "Boatbuilder Laureate of the Maine Coast." These public acknowledgments of his contributions are richly deserved.

On a personal level, I am grateful for the opportunity I've had to watch him at work, for his willingness to share his knowledge and insights with me, and—most of all—for the chance to get to know him as a great artist, a great craftsman, and a great friend.

What follows is Ralph's story, in his own words, which I've distilled by organizing and editing the material from our many hours of discussion. I hope you will enjoy getting to know Ralph Stanley as much as I have.

—Craig S. Milner
Worcester, Massachusetts
March 1, 2004

CHAPTER *One*

MY FATHER WAS A FISHERMAN

I've always made sure when I built a boat that it would give shelter, and there's a good reason for that.

My father once had a little lobster boat, a double-ender that was built on Cranberry Island back before 1920, I believe. It didn't have a cabin. It was just an open boat with a spray hood on the bow. Originally it had a make-and-break engine, but at that time it had a four-cylinder Kermath.

One day back in January 1934 when I hadn't quite turned five years old, he was out lobstering. It looked like it was about ready to snow at any time. The weather was overcast, but it was calm and fairly cold. Along towards the end of the day, my father was on his way in through the gut at Cranberry Island. The generator had quit working, so the battery ran down and, of course, the engine stopped.

Then it started to breeze up northwest, and it snowed some in the night after the wind came. My father got awfully cold, and he was adrift. Nobody saw him and it got dark, so he put some gasoline and rags in a bucket on the stern deck and lit it. He let it burn, and the lifesaving station at Islesford and the lighthouse on Baker's Island saw these flares.

He was right close in to Islesford, but the thirty-six-foot lifeboat they could have used to rescue him was hauled out. All they had was a twenty-five-foot lighthouse tender. That was an open boat with a spray hood on it, and it only had a

The double-ender that my father went adrift in.

little four-cylinder engine. When they tried to go out, it iced up and they had to turn back.

My father kept drifting, and the wind was breezing up more all the time. After a few hours the people at Duck Island Light, about ten miles out, could see his flares. The lifesaving station at Baker's Island could still see them, too, but they waited and waited and didn't go out to get him. Finally, Mount Desert Rock, about twenty miles out, could see his flares as the night went on.

The wind was northwest, and the water got pretty choppy; his boat was just drifting. My father put out an anchor, but he was drifting off so fast that it couldn't reach bottom and catch hold, although it did keep him into the wind somewhat. The boat rolled so much from side to side that he had to wedge himself between the engine box and the side of the boat just to stay in her. Sometimes she'd roll right down to her rails.

My father had no heat aboard of her and it was cold and he kept drifting. The temperature got down to five below zero that night, and to keep warm he kept his arms moving and his muscles working by sawing a handline over the rails. He knew he shouldn't go to sleep. I've always thought about that and made sure when I built a boat that it would give shelter.

My mother, of course, was frantic. I remember going to bed that night, and he hadn't got in. Roby Norwood came to the house and took my mother down to Seawall to see if they could see anything. But they couldn't. And there were different people calling in, being worried and everything.

My mother had been calling the lifesaving station and getting no action from them. They said they were doing all they could. Finally, along about midnight, she called the captain of the *Kickapoo*. That was an icebreaker stationed in Rockland to keep the Penobscot River open.

The *Kickapoo* was steam powered. The captain told my mother it would take about four hours to get up steam, but he would go just as soon as he could. He left Rockland about four o'clock in the morning and got to Mount Desert

Rock about eight, just as Clarence Harding had found my father and taken him in tow.

My father had drifted all night long, and Clarence was going out lobstering from Bass Harbor. Someone told him, "Look out for Chester Stanley. He's out there adrift somewhere." Well, my father's anchor had fetched up on a shoal called the No'the'n Peak. It was just inside of Mount Desert Rock. That's where Clarence found him, and the water was rough.

The first thing Clarence did was get alongside, close enough to throw my father a dinner pail so he'd have something hot to drink and eat. Then the *Kickapoo* showed up, and they saw that Clarence had my father in tow and that everything was okay. So, they turned around and went back to Rockland.

I don't know how the *Kickapoo* would have taken him in tow anyway, because she was almost two hundred feet long. They might have had to launch a boat to go get him. My father might have had to leave his boat there. It's lucky that he did fetch up on the Peak, because otherwise he'd have kept going right out to sea.

Anyway, Clarence towed a life preserver on a rope by my father's boat so he could pick it up. Then my father put a buoy on his anchor and left it right there. Clarence took him in tow, and just outside the Western Way a boat from Cranberry Island took over. They towed his boat up here to Southwest Harbor.

My mother had got word that he was on his way. She went down to the dock, but they towed his boat up empty. That scared her to death! It turned out they'd dropped my father off at Cranberry Island and had filled him full of whiskey there. He got home finally and it had snowed in the night and I remember that he took my sister Ruth and me on sleds and dragged us all around town. He probably had so much whiskey in him that if he'd stayed home he'd have just gone to sleep!

Well, the lifesaving station on Islesford all got shaken up and transferred, and they brought in a new crew. They shouldn't have had that lifeboat hauled out without having a relief boat to take its place. The captain of the *Kickapoo* wanted my mother to write him a letter and tell it all to justify their coming out, so she did.

That sea is powerful, and so is the weather. Everybody thought my father was gone, because it was so cold and the wind blew a gale. If my father had laid down in the bow of his boat, he'd have frozen to death. As it was, his fingers got frostbitten.

When my father was a boy, his brother had come down across three of his fingers with an ax and cut them almost completely off. They were just hanging by the skin. Someone wrapped his hand up in a towel and rushed him to Northeast Harbor, where there was a doctor staying for the summer, and he put them back together.

But after that experience of being frostbitten out there in January, my father would lose the circulation in his fingers quite easy, and they always bothered him somewhat after that. He was about thirty-five, I guess, when he went adrift. If he'd been older, he probably wouldn't have made it.

CHAPTER *Two*

VISITING AUNT ALICE

Ever since I can remember, I was drawing pictures of boats, and one person who encouraged me when I was a boy was Aunt Alice Gilley. She was my great-grandmother's sister, and she was quite a character.

She was actually a relative on both sides of my family. In one way she was my great-aunt and in another way she was my great-great-aunt. She didn't get married until late in life, and when she did it was to a relative of hers, Charles B. Gilley. He was a Civil War veteran, and he was blind. I think it was from the Civil War days. She was his third wife, and she had a baby by him, but the baby died.

I know she liked boys, and I used to think it was great to go up there and see her, but she was awfully dirty. Everything was nasty. She only washed the dishes once a week. By this time Charles B. Gilley had died, and there was this old fella named Pat Osborne who was a boarder there. When they would have their lunch, they'd take a piece of bread, wipe the plate out clean with it, eat the bread, and wash it down with a cup of tea. That was their dessert. When they got done eating, they just hauled a cloth over the table to keep the flies off, and it was all set for the next meal.

When we went to visit, Aunt Alice always wanted to give me something to eat, but my mother would feed me up beforehand with candy

Aunt Alice

on winter afternoons it would be cold with the wind blowing down across Norwood's Cove. They'd go by her house, she'd see them coming, and she'd call to them. "Come on in, boys," she'd say, and she'd throw half a dozen biscuits in the oven and heat them up in good shape, good and crusty, and hot.

She'd take them out and put some butter on them and give them to the boys. Henry Dunbar was recalling about it one time, and he said, "Those biscuits were some good! But when you stop and think about it, gosh, she was some nasty! But we never got sick." Well, baking those biscuits at about four hundred and fifty degrees would kill anything!

Aunt Alice wasn't much for gossip. One time, she was with a bunch of women from around town at some club or a meeting they were having, and they were running down this girl that had gotten pregnant. And Aunt Alice says, "Oh, don't run the poor girl down. It could have been any one of you, and you know it!" And they shut right up.

Then another time, she bought some matches in Anse Holmes's store and took them home, and they wouldn't light. So she brought them back to Anse and says, "These matches are no good. They won't light."

"That's funny," he says, and he opened the box and took one out and scratched it on his pants and it lit first thing. Anse used to wear these old blue serge suits, and they were all shiny from dirt. "Well, I don't see anything wrong with them," he says.

and cake and cookies and sweet stuff, so I was full when I got there and didn't want anything to eat.

Aunt Alice smoked a TD pipe. They were popular in those days, made out of clay and baked in an oven. The TD was short and white, like white enamel, and it had a mouthpiece fitted on it. Aunt Alice had an ashtray on her windowsill, and she never smoked her pipe when you went in. It might be on the windowsill still smoking, but she wouldn't touch it while you were there. She also would hand me these little cigars to give to my father.

Aunt Alice was always good to the boys in town. They used to walk home from school, and

Now, the store was full of people, and Aunt Alice says, "Well! I didn't know I had to scratch them on my ass."

She was quite a character all right.

But Aunt Alice always had these pictures of ships, square-riggers, that came off of rope calendars in those days. She always had them hanging on the walls, and I liked that. So I used to go up and look at them. Then I'd go home and draw pictures for her and color them with crayons.

I couldn't have been much more than four years old when I did this. I'd take them up to her, and she'd pin them up on the wall with her other ship pictures. They stayed right there, and they were still hanging on the wall when she died.

CHAPTER *Three*

GOING TO LOOK AT BOATS

I always liked to go out looking at boats. Sometimes my mother would hire a babysitter, and my sister and I would get the babysitter to take us up to Norwood's Cove to see the four-masted schooner *Theoline* anchored out there for the winter.

And when I was about five or six years old—before I went to school—I'd get my father to take us on rides to go around and look at boats.

He owned an old 1924 Essex automobile that he'd had even before he was married. Lyle Newman had owned it, and he had sold it to my great-uncle, William D. Stanley, who was known as Uncle Jimmy or Pa Jim, for eight hundred dollars. It was down here at Clark Point, and Lyle

showed him how to get it going and run it.

Uncle Jimmy lived over to Manset at that time, and he ran the car up the road, made the corner uptown perfect, and went over and made Manset corner all right. He drove it in the driveway, and there was a barn out there with the door open. So he drove the Essex into the barn, right through the back wall, and out the other side! It got hung up, and the front of the car was sticking out through the back of the barn.

My father was in the house with Aunt Nan, and they heard this crash and went outside to see what had happened. By that time, Uncle Jimmy had gotten out and was standing there scratching his head. The front wheels were still

Uncle Jimmy

time. It was a nice-riding car, as I remember. It rode like a baby carriage, had nice springs.

Behind the rear seat there was a heater that took heat from the exhaust, and my father was always scared of that. Those heaters could leak and asphyxiate you. People got gassed that way. But my father was always awful careful of it. It was never any problem.

That car also had mechanical brakes, and you had to adjust them all the time. That was a bad feature of the Essex. Before you went anywhere you had to adjust the brakes. My mother never would drive it, but my grandmother was quite venturesome, and she drove that car to Ellsworth one time. My father held onto the emergency brake all the way, but she did fine.

Anyway, we'd take the old Essex down to the point or over to Bass Harbor or Manset to look at the boats. I liked to study old boats that were worn out and hauled up on the shore, just falling to pieces. That's one thing you don't see much nowadays. Once people find an old boat on the beach, they think it's unsightly and they've got to get rid of it.

Back in the old days, there was a schooner that was hauled up here at Clark Cove. She was dying, falling to pieces. The masts were out of her, and she was just a wreck.

Some of the local people started thinking that old schooner was an eyesore, that this was a terrible thing for the summer people to see when they got off at the steamboat wharf and went up to the hotels. So they decided they ought to get rid of that unsightly old wreck, and

spinning. Uncle Jimmy looked up to see my father and he says, "Ches, if you can get her out of there, she's your'n."

So that was the car my father had when I was a little boy. We used to go in it to Ellsworth and other places, and I remember riding to Bangor to go Christmas shopping in it—my mother, my grandmother, my father, my sister, and I. That Essex had an aluminum-block engine and big tires with wooden-spoke wheels and a big, square Fisher body with two doors, the same body that Buick used. Even the steering wheel was wood. It was a pretty good car for the day. I can't remember when my father last had it on the road, but maybe it was in the '30s some

Aunt Nan

they hired a man to come and take it apart. He could have what he got out of it, the wood or the fastenings or whatever. Well, it was a tougher job than he expected, and he gave it up. Finally they floated her out on a ledge and set her afire and burned her. They got the metal out of her, and that was it.

When the summer people came the next year, they were terribly disappointed that the old wreck was gone. They had liked to sit and make sketches or paint pictures of her, and their subject was gone!

But I always used to go around and hunt for old boats like that. I used to like to see how they were constructed and study the model of them. I'd think about what they were used for and where they'd been.

And when I got big enough to walk around town by myself, I used to go down to Clark Point here and look out across at the boats on their moorings in the harbor. I was always looking at boats.

CHAPTER Four

MY GRANDMOTHER'S HOUSE

I grew up in my grandmother's house in Southwest Harbor. She was my mother's mother, and her name was Celestia Dix. She came from Bartlett's Island, just off the western side of Mount Desert Island, and married my grandfather, Ralph Robinson, about 1898. They lived in that house with my great-grandfather, Adoniram Judson Robinson, who was named for a famous missionary to India, and my great-grandmother, Henrietta (Clark) Robinson.

My great-grandfather was called Jud, and he was a sea captain. He built that house in something like 1866 and brought up his family there. I was always told that he had steered a vessel to Boston when he was nine years old. He went to

sea with his father, Levi Robinson, who was also a captain, and spent his life at sea. He used to go down to the Caribbean and South America on coasting schooners.

My great-grandfather and his father owned the schooner *Pilot* and also the schooner *Brilliant* back in the 1850s. Sometimes I find one name listed in the Customs records as owner, and sometimes the other. They probably used those vessels in fishing or coasting.

I've also found records from the 1870s showing that my great-grandfather was master of the two-masted schooner *Gamecock*. She was built over in Bar Harbor, and he may have owned shares in her, too. There are old newspaper

*My grandmother, Celestia (Dix) Robinson
in the late 1940s or early 1950s.*

accounts saying the *Gamecock* was going back and forth between Calais, in Maine, and Boston, Danvers, and Lynn, in Massachusetts, quite regularly. Sometimes she even went to New York.

In 1882, the *Gamecock* was sold to Nova Scotia parties, and A. J. Robinson became master of a three-masted schooner named the *Andrew Nebinger* that was even bigger. When I was young, there was an old fella named Artemus Richardson who was a relative of mine. He told me that he remembered my great-grandfather and that vessel. He said my great-grandfather kept that schooner like a yacht, and consequently he got good fares with her and good-paying cargo, and he made quite a lot of money with her.

Back when Artemus was a boy himself, the schooners would be down at the wharf unloading

coal, and my great-grandfather would let the boys come aboard of his vessel. They'd climb the rigging, and he'd let the kids do anything. He had a good way with them. Then when he needed something done, the boys would turn to and help him. He probably paid them a little something, or maybe the cook gave them a biscuit out of the galley.

Sometimes there would be another schooner alongside, but her master, Captain Lunt, wouldn't let the boys aboard of his vessel. He'd drive them off. So they used to think up tricks to play on old Captain Lunt. And Artemus remembers, "What we couldn't think of, your great-grandfather could. He'd set the boys up to doing things, and then he'd sit back and chuckle."

My grandmother used to say that her father-in-law was easy to get along with but that her mother-in-law, Henrietta, wasn't. One time, Henrietta decided that her husband was too old to go to sea. So she got on the steamboat and went to Bangor to see Fred Ayer, who was the principal owner of my great-grandfather's vessel. She wanted Mr. Ayer to fire him.

Mr. Ayer told her, no, he couldn't. My great-grandfather had been a captain for a good many years and he'd made them a lot of money. As long as they had a vessel and Jud wanted to go to sea, he was sure of having a vessel to sail. My great-grandfather was in his sixties at this point, maybe sixty-five or so. He was captain of the *Andrew Nebinger* until he retired in 1909 or 1910.

When he was at sea, he walked the quarter-

My great-grandfather, A. J. Robinson, had this photo of the Andrew Nebinger. *It was taken in Stonington, Connecticut, in the early 1900s while she was there for repairs after being run into. (Damage to the hull can be seen below the first mast.)*

deck back and forth. It was just a habit, I guess, and when he retired, he walked back and forth on the big porch that ran across the front of the house, no matter what the weather. And that porch never had a roof on it, either.

My great-grandfather had already passed away by the time I was born. I think he was seventy-four when he died in 1912, and the house he built went to my grandfather, Ralph Robinson, who was a painter. He painted many houses around town, and he was good at signs, too. He also painted the fancy scrolls people had on their

carriages in those days. There were lots of horse-drawn carriages around. The summer people brought them here. They were real finely crafted and all had fancy pinstripes. They were highly varnished, and they'd shine like a piano.

Beside my grandparents' house there was a barn where my grandfather would take these carriages in and sand them down and get them all prepared to refinish. He'd dust and dust for days before he'd varnish. Conditions had to be just right. When he was varnishing, he didn't allow anybody in the barn at all. He'd get out there and

27

My mother, Bertha Robinson, at an early age.

varnish a carriage, and there wouldn't be a speck on it when he got done, not an imperfection anywhere. It would come out perfect.

The wheel spokes had pinstripes on them, too. My grandfather had a brush called a striper that he'd come down the spoke with and shutter it off to a fine point. The stripe would start out as a teardrop but it would end up real long—the whole length of the spoke—and taper almost to nothing at the end. The wheels had a stripe, too. He'd put the wheel in the vise and give it a spin. Then he'd put his striper on it and spin the stripe all the way around it.

Even though he didn't go to sea, my grandfather must have been out on the water at some time, with his father being a captain and all, and he did have an interest in ships. I've seen some pictures of vessels that he'd drawn in his schoolbooks, just with a pencil, and I think he could have been quite an artist.

My grandfather died in 1924. He had been quite sick, and my mother, Bertha, came home and took care of him that winter. She was my grandparents' only child, and she had been away at the Massachusetts General Hospital in Boston, training to be a nurse.

I don't know what he actually had, but because he was a painter, they treated him for lead poisoning. They gave him arsenic. That was the treatment for lead poisoning in those days, and the treatment would kill you if the lead poisoning didn't. The doctor told my mother he did not have cancer, but I wonder. He was only in his fifties.

After he died, my mother went back and finished her training. She worked for a while as a supervisor at a maternity hospital near Boston, and then she came home to Southwest Harbor and stayed in the family house. I don't know whether she ever worked in a hospital around here or not, but I do know she did private nursing for people. She and my father, Chester Stanley, were married in Ellsworth on November 8, 1926, by Reverend. A. T. Bradstreet.

The house went to my grandmother, and it was hers as long as I was growing up. I was born in Bar Harbor Hospital on February 9, 1929. I was the oldest and I had seven sisters, so it was pretty much a house full of girls. We were all about two years apart, and they kept coming along as I grew up. There was a big family of us, and everybody was working. My grandmother worked, too. She was quite an enterprising woman. In 1902, she was listed in a book as one of the leading businesswomen in Southwest Harbor. My grandmother ran the telephone office and had the switchboard in her house. She was quite clever, and she was quite mechanical, too.

After my grandfather died, she told Jones Wass, who owned the sardine factory here in town, that she thought she'd go down and pack sardines. And he says, "No, I won't hire you. I don't want you down there with those women. They're a tough crowd, and you're too gentle to be down there with them."

Those women *were* pretty tough, and if they didn't get the sardines they wanted and had to hold up a minute, they'd swear at the tenders. My grandmother was awful disappointed that Jones Wass wouldn't give her a job, but afterwards I guess she was glad he didn't. Even though he wouldn't hire her in the factory, he always brought her his sewing work, like suits that had to be fixed and pants that had to be shortened or lengthened. So he gave her a lot of work that way.

To get by, my grandmother rented rooms in the house, and she altered dresses for summer people, which she'd done even before my grandfather died. I think she started doing that around 1910, and the styles kept getting shorter from then on into the 1930s. Almost as late as 1940 she was still shortening some of the same dresses she'd first altered in 1910.

A portrait of me taken at Osgood's Studio in Ellsworth.

In the summer, these big black limousines would pull up out in front of the house, and the chauffeur would get out, all dressed up with his gloves on. He'd let this lady out and stand at attention by the car while she went inside and got fitted. I used to like to go out and look those limousines over.

When the Civilian Conservation Corps, the CCC, came to town in the 1930s, the government outfitted all the young fellas with World War I army clothes that they had left over. These were nice suits and work clothes, but of course they didn't fit, so the fellas would bring them to my grandmother to make cuffs and things like that.

Then during World War II, the Coast Guard down at Clark Point and the navy base at Seawall brought uniforms to her to be altered, and that kept her pretty busy. Many nights I went to sleep hearing that old sewing machine whirring away, and listening to the sound of the foot pedal. She'd be sewing way into the wee hours of the morning sometimes. My grandmother also did all the alterations for Pete Somes, who owned the men's clothing store that was in the Odd Fellows block here in town.

When I was a kid, we had some bouts of sickness, and we caught scarlet fever one winter. I was about ten years old and I got it first, but it went through the whole family. There were five or six of us then, and each one of us came down with scarlet fever just about six weeks apart. My grandmother and my father had already had it. But my mother hadn't, and she got it. It kept us sick all winter long. In those times, they quarantined everybody with scarlet fever, and we were quarantined all winter. People walked on the other side of the street, scared to death.

At that time my grandmother was sick with something else, and times were hard. You couldn't go out and get to the store. Sometimes a neighbor would go by, and we'd leave some money out on the porch and holler at him. He'd come and take the money and get what we needed and bring it back and leave it on the porch and run!

Once the quarantine was over, everything had to be fumigated. At that time, Artemus Richardson was the town health officer, and he had to come and burn formaldehyde in the house to get the disease out. Nowadays, they wouldn't do that, but that's what they thought they had to do. My mother was told to burn up a lot of books that she had—her nursing books and children's books and clothes they thought should be destroyed.

Back then, there was no TV, of course, so we read a lot. My grandfather Robinson had kept books in the house, too, and those had to get burned up. It was rough to lose all that stuff, but when times were hardest like that, it seemed the family was closest together.

CHAPTER *Five*

MY BOUT WITH PNEUMONIA

One Saturday in November of 1942, when I was thirteen years old and in the eighth grade, I'd been down on the Manset fish wharf baiting trawls with my father. I got one tub about half done in the morning, and I didn't feel good. I tried to finish it, but I guessed I'd better give it up. I put a bag over the bait and left it and went home.

I was home for a few days and sat around and didn't go to school. Come Thanksgiving, I had my Thanksgiving dinner, but I still didn't feel so good. This went on for another week or more after that, and then I came down with pneumonia.

When we were sick we used to go in the back

room. There was a couch to lie on and a wood-stove to keep you warm. Well, I got worse and worse, and my father had to lug me upstairs to my own bed. There was a stove up in that room, too, and they kept the fire going and got the doctor.

Dr. Hagopian was Armenian, and his parents were killed in the war with the Turks. In fact, I think he saw them killed. I don't know how he got to this country, but he ended up over here and went to medical school and became a doctor. He had come to Southwest Harbor in the CCC back in the 1930s, and then later he set up practice here in town. He came down and checked me over, and sure enough, I had pneumonia.

This was now into the first part of December. There was snow on the ground, I remember, and it was cold. One night I was awful sick. I had these coughing spells. I'd strangle and gag and throw up nothing but phlegm. I was just as weak as a rag. I could hardly pick myself up off the bed.

Now, in those days when you had pneumonia, you always went through a crisis. You'd either get well or you'd die. So the doctor said, "He'll have his crisis tonight."

That night—it must have been eleven o'clock or so—I had this awful coughing spell, and I was all in. I just plopped back down on the bed. And then I remember, all of a sudden, there was a big light. I wasn't scared or anything. I knew I was going to die, but it was like coming out of a storm into a calm. Everything was perfect. I felt fine, and there was no pain.

I don't know whether I was in a tunnel or not, like people say. It seemed as if I was in something, and there was a big light at the end. I was conscious of some beings there, and they were communicating with me from beyond the light. But it wasn't words. There was no speaking. It was whole thoughts that came from them to me, and my thoughts went right to them, and it was just as natural as could be. I can remember thinking, "Boy, this is great."

There was a question as to whether I should go back, and I thought, "No, I don't want to go back. This is fun. Can we keep going?"

Well, there was more debate amongst these beings, and I couldn't understand what was going on. Finally I was thinking, "I want to go, but I can't. I've got to stay because my mother and father and grandmother and all my sisters are working so hard to keep me alive. I can't go. I've got to go back."

Then it was decided that I *would* go back, and they also had the idea that there was something for me to do. I don't know what it was. They didn't tell me. And I was not conscious of the light going out or my coming back. But the next thing, I was back, and the storm was over.

When I woke up again in bed, I still didn't feel good, of course. I felt like I'd been dragged through a knothole. I had no strength at all, but they said that's when the color came back in my face.

Finally, I got well. After Christmas vacation I went back to school, but they told me not to overdo it. That first morning, I was tired at noontime, so I didn't go back that afternoon. I thought I'd go the next day, but then I was worse, and the following day I was worse still. I'd had a relapse, and I had to go back to bed.

The doctor came down again and checked me over, and this time he said I had pleurisy. He took a tape and measured my chest to the midpoint from one side and then around the other way to the midpoint. I was something like an inch-and-a-half bigger on one side than the other. The pleural cavity was all full of fluid. Today, they would just stick a needle in there and tap it out, but Dr. Hagopian didn't want to do it.

At first it looked like I'd have to go to the hospital. In those days it was a hard trip, and they took you in the hearse, which was gray and doubled as the ambulance. They'd just change the sign in the window, and it had a siren they'd blow. Otherwise, you might go in somebody's car if they had one available. But the doctor didn't want to put me through that, so he kept me home and they used hot-water bottles and turned me from side to side. That kept the fluid from settling in one place. I finally pulled out of that, but at the same time I had a mastoid abscess in both ears. That's why one ear is a bit deaf today. They gave me a sulfa drug, and they credited that with saving me.

Eventually I felt better, but I didn't get out of the house until the first of March, which was too late to go back to school that year. They decided it would be best for me to rest and take it easy and go back the next year and take that grade over again.

So I had a lot of time to think about boats, and I kept busy designing and drawing out plans. Harvey Kelly, who lived across the street, was teaching school in Southwest, and he had copies of magazines like *Yachting*, *Motor Boating*, and *Rudder* that he brought over for me to look at. In those times, there were boat plans in those magazines, and I got a lot out of studying the designs and pictures. That was quite an influence on me.

One thing that I used to follow in *Motor Boating* was the "Traditions and Memories of American Yachting." That was really good, and I read it whenever I could scrape up enough money to buy the magazine. Another publication I read quite often was called the *Fishing Gazette*. That carried articles about the older draggers and fishing boats from the 1930s and back to the 1920s. It even had pictures of interesting boats like schooners that were converted to draggers.

I read a lot of books, too, some of them several times. There weren't many that told you much about boat design, not that I could get hold of anyway in those times. I did read L. Francis Herreshoff's books, and I learned an awful lot about design just by studying those and the magazines, so I made good use of the time while I was sick.

By April or May of 1943, I could get out on my bicycle, and I used to go down to the town dock. I'd pull up against the southwestern side of a little building they had and just sit on my bike and look out at the boats. It was nice and warm there in the sun in the spring.

I'd also go over to Manset, to the fish wharf. Many of the working vessels that I had read about came in at some point and tied up. There were plenty of old boats, too, and they were interesting to look at.

CHAPTER *Six*

MY TEACHERS

When I was a little kid, I was always building some kind of a boat to float in a pond or a puddle. My mother always encouraged me, and I used to take these models down to the shore and sail them just to see how they'd float. Looking back at the old boatbuilders that I can remember, they all did the same thing when they were boys.

I had used planes and hammers and saws even then. It was mostly just by myself, playing. I used to go up to the grocery store and get orange crates and make stuff out of them. Some of it was kind of crude, but it was practice. Then when I was in the seventh grade I started taking shop class, and that was where I really got started with many of the skills I've used as a boatbuilder all these years.

The class was in the new high-school building they had put up here in Southwest Harbor a few years before. We had a teacher named Albert Barlow who came from Boothbay Harbor, and he was a great teacher. I really learned a great deal from him about mechanical drawing and doing boat lines, and also about woodworking. We learned how to sharpen tools and keep things properly. In his shop, everything was in its place—perfect and sharp and kept good.

I can remember him standing up in front of the class with his shop coat on. When the boys were getting a little unruly, he'd say, "There'll be no more horseplay today!"

We had fun in the shop, though, too. I shared a bench with another fellow, who was left-

This is me at about five years old (left) with my friend Bob Bannister in a picture his grandfather took at Long Pond.

pine boards. We had to plane those boards down and stain and varnish them. Then we put hinges on them, and there were a couple of bolts that went through the holes in the paper. I was quite surprised at what I did in those days.

Barlow also taught adult-education courses, and the men around town could go in the evenings. They built some nice cabinets and furniture. I can remember going to the gymnasium, to the shows of what the young students had made and of what the adults had made. It was impressive. Some of those men became the Hinckley Company's best finish carpenters.

Barlow was an awfully good teacher, exceptional. He was fussy. He wanted things done right. I think the desire to do things right was something I got from him, too, aside from the practical skills. I had a certain amount of wanting to do things right in me anyway, but he showed me how.

The principal of the high school, Carroll Ronco, was another one that I learned a great deal from. He taught me algebra and geometry. We had a class reunion a few years ago, and he remembered me. He says, "You were pretty sharp in that geometry class. You knew what was going on all the time."

And I said, "Well, I had a pretty good teacher."

handed and awful clumsy. I had a vise on my end of the bench and he had one on his end. We were supposed to square up some boards, and Barlow would come by and check our work. My board would usually be okay, but this other fella couldn't get his square to save his life. He'd grab his plane and go down the board with it, and things just wouldn't be straight. It'd be off to one side, twisted. Our teacher would shake his head and put the board down and go on to the next bench.

While Barlow was turned around, this fellow would put his board back in the vise. I'd grab my plane and just give it two or three swipes real quick and go back to my work. He'd unclamp it and run down to catch Barlow and get him to check it. Sometimes it'd be all right, and sometimes it wouldn't. We thought we were getting away with something, but I bet Barlow knew what was going on. When I think back on it, I'm *sure* he knew it.

A while ago I found some work that I had done in Barlow's shop. It was a little notebook with wooden covers that we had to make out of

CHAPTER Seven

LOCAL BOATBUILDING

There's always been quite a history of shipbuilding and boatbuilding right here on Mount Desert Island. Of course, in the old days, it was all hand work building those big vessels. There were no power tools.

They usually had a half model to build big ships with, and they would have used a half model for regular boats, too. There were formulas and methods for widening a big vessel or lengthening it, and they'd use the half model and mechanical measuring devices to scale it up. Or they could alter those models by eye, as they saw fit.

A lot of small-boat construction went on, too, but there's not much of a written record about who the builders were or what they did. I do know that a man named Andrew Haynes of Manset built some nice rowboats. As a matter of fact, I've got one of them, and it's over a hundred years old.

In those days, all the builders worked from half models or from plans in their heads. There wouldn't be a drawing or anything written, and they just built with whatever materials they had at hand. If the lumber for the stem had a good curve to it, they'd put the good curve in. If it didn't have such a good curve, they'd put that piece in anyway. They made do with what they had.

I don't know exactly when the summer people started to have boats built locally. I imagine they started thinking they might have a boat built to use here about the time they started having cottages built. But at first, they brought their own boats up here, boats that had been built elsewhere.

Some people brought catboats. It was all sailing boats then, since small engines were not available yet, and they were mostly gaff rigged. In those days, a sloop was called either a "sloopboat" or a "yacht boat" or sometimes just a yacht.

I found an old newspaper article where Clarence Clark, my grandfather's cousin, had a sloopboat that was named the *Annie Bess* for his two daughters. She was a Friendship design, and I imagine he used her for sailing summer people that were staying at the Island House or the Claremont.

Back around the turn of the century, Professor Charles Eliot of Harvard was staying at Northeast Harbor. He was having Lewis Freeman Gott build him a sloop at Bass Harbor, and the newspaper said that it was being built to Professor Eliot's specifications. Well, the next year, there was an article in the paper saying that Lewis Freeman Gott was building *another* boat for Professor Eliot, the one from the year before having proved "not sufficient." This time, Gott was building the boat to his own specifications. Forget what the professor wanted. He was building it the way it *ought* to be built.

At that time, summer people chartered the local sailboats, which were fishing boats from Cranberry Island, to go on excursions. And there were races. Lewis Freeman Gott entered all he could get into. I found an account of a race sponsored by the Northeast Harbor summer people, one that he entered in his centerboard sloop named the *Merry Wings*.

Then there was a little community called Dirigo, on Butter Island in east Penobscot Bay, and they used to sponsor a sloop race. They'd get boats from Castine, Deer Isle, and Bucks Harbor. Gott always entered that one, too. There's a cup over in the Tremont Historical Society, and it's inscribed with the names of all the sloops that won that race. Gott won three years in a row, so he got to keep the cup.

After the turn of the century you got more powerboats. Again, some of the summer people brought theirs with them or had them shipped up from New York or Philadelphia. But there were also power boats being built on Cranberry Island, and some of the summer people put in orders.

At first these boats had naphtha engines. They boiled the naphtha and used that in a condenser, like you would steam, and reused it and reused it. They also burned naphtha for the fuel. But naphtha was scary stuff, and those engines were dangerous. They blew up sometimes.

I had a great-uncle that built boats here back at the turn of the century. His name was John C. Ralph, and he was married to my grandmother's sister, Etherlinda Dix. He was into everything. At one time, he was postmaster, had a bicycle shop, and had a photography studio right in the middle of town, where Sawyer's Market is now. He also was a carpenter and built houses.

Old sloops sailing off the Rock End Hotel dock at Gilpatrick Cove, with Great Cranberry Island in the background.

He built some sloops here in the 1890s. I found a newspaper article where he had rented his own boat to parties in Seal Harbor or Northeast Harbor, and he was starting to build another one for himself. It was called his "yacht." Then, after the turn of the century, when naphtha launches came in, my great-uncle built some of those, and I believe he built a few gasoline launches, too. Chances are he built some of those for the summer people.

Back in the 1890s, there was a fella named William Keene. He lived over at Manset and built quite a number of steam launches, maybe six or seven. They were about thirty-six feet long. He built one for a man named Hadlock down at Islesford, and he built another one that he used himself here in town. When the schooners used to come in with coal, he'd tow them in to the coal wharf with those little steam launches.

He also used to run excursion parties around the harbor with those steamers. As a matter of fact, Gertrude Whitmore Carroll's journal tells about going on an excursion to Brooklin and back in one of William Keene's steam launches.

Then along came the make-and-break engine, and those were safer and more economical. They were two-cycle, where you had to mix the oil with the gasoline, and they didn't last too long. They had to have new bearings put in them and stuff like that, but they could be fixed quite easily.

When I was boy, there were always boats being built in town, and they were all wood. Before World War II, it was pretty much the old-timers that were building boats, and, with the exception of Hinckley's and Southwest Boat, the boat shops were quite small then. Nobody had heard of fiberglass.

A good boat would last twenty-five or thirty

The schooner William Keene *at Manset fish wharf circa 1941 in a photo taken by Southwest Harbor photographer W. H. (Bill) Ballard.*

years, but generally they had to have some work done on them when they got to be about fifteen. Most of the lobstermen that were doing well would keep a boat for fifteen years, sell it, and get another one. Boats were cheap in those days.

There was no boatbuilding school, so all the newcomers pretty much learned from the older builders. But a lot of them didn't know how to teach. You'd go and ask them a question about how they did such-and-such, and they didn't know how to tell you. They could do it, but they couldn't tell you *how* they did it, and usually the builders wanted to keep it that way. It was protecting their job. Back then, a man that could build a boat was regarded as *somebody*. It was something special.

Down at the Cranberry Islands they built double-enders, pretty much a certain model, a little different than anywhere else. Great Cranberry Island had a particular style. You could see one and know where it came from. They were all good boats.

Around to Bass Harbor, the Riches were building boats, and over in Bar Harbor there were boatbuilders, too. Fred Hayes, who had sightseeing boats, built some over there. But I think boatbuilding was more concentrated here in Southwest Harbor than elsewhere on the island. And all the builders had their own methods, the way they did things. Everybody had their little quirks.

Sim Mayo built boats down here on Clark Point, where Southwest Boat was later, and he had different people work for him. Then he sold out to Andrew Parker, but Parker hired people to build boats. He didn't build them himself.

Chester Clement bought the place in 1929, I think it was. He had built boats up here in town, in a building that Will Herrick owned on the corner of Cedar Lane. The *Leader*, the boat that my father sailed the Neilsons in, was built there. But that building's gone now. They tore it down a few years ago. There wasn't much height inside, but there was room enough to build a boat. In those days, the builders didn't put cabins on them. They were all open boats, fitted with spray hoods. And that worked fine until later on, when people wanted shelters. Then the builders had to make the boats higher.

So Chester Clement bought the boat works just around the time the Depression started, and I think some of the first vessels he built were rum runners. One was eighty feet long and sixteen feet wide and had three airplane engines in it. It had armor plate on it, too. It had a little pilothouse with those little narrow windows like a Brinks truck, and a flush deck. It was registered for fishing, but I don't know how much fishing they ever did with it.

Chester did build fishing boats, too, including a thirty-four-footer for Harvard Beal in 1931, one that my father owned later. Around that time, Harvard had an older boat that was leaking quite badly. He was fishing off Mount Desert Rock and he decided he needed something newer, so he came in and ordered one. Twenty-one days later, he was back off the Rock in his new boat, fishing. She had a Van Blerk in her. That was a pop-

This is the boat Chester Clement built for Harvard Beal, the one that my father owned later (photo from about 1947, the year of the great Bar Harbor fire).

ular marine engine at the time, quite big and powerful. She'd go good with it. Harvard had her until 1935 or '36, when my father bought her.

They had built her quick and had nailed the planks in the hull right to the floor timbers. Coming in from Mount Desert Rock one time, Harvard gave her a pounding and pulled a nail right through one of the planks. My father had that hole plugged when he owned the boat, but every once in a while she'd work and the nail head would push the plug out and she'd start leaking again. Finally, he had to nail a lath over that plug to hold it in. It was still there when he sold her.

My father owned that thirty-four-footer for thirty-five years or more. He'd had new floor timbers put in her because he was going haking in her and needed the platform solid to hold the weight of the catch. That's what probably saved her.

I was only eight in 1937, when Chester Clement was killed in an automobile accident, but he was the first boatbuilder I can remember being aware of. I didn't have any personal contact with him, but I can remember a lot of the work that he did. They said he was a whiz at planking up a boat and could do it in no time. After working on my own boats, I can appreciate what he did and how he did it.

It was too bad Chester Clement died early. If he'd lived up into the war years, he probably could have had military contracts, and the boat works would have really done well. Maybe he and Henry Hinckley would have gotten together. But he died, and Hinckley and Lennox "Bing" Sargent bought the place. During the war, Hinckley's yard and Southwest Boat were all one company.

About the time the war started, Hinckley had a contract to build eight or nine sailing yawls for the Naval Academy, and then they got contracts to build thirty-eight-foot picket boats for the Coast Guard. The government elected to make them out of wood because steel was scarce and they needed it for the big vessels.

Hinckley was also building twenty-six-foot mine yawls for the army. Those were strictly motorboats; the army just called them yawls. They had a little shelter on the front with a windshield and canvas over it, but they were mostly open and meant for harbor-patrol work and tending mines and that sort of thing. The yard built some forty-six-foot tugboats, too, and they even made some that had tunnel sterns. I believe those were used in the Amazon River. The bottom was hollowed up in, and the propeller was up high so they wouldn't draw much water.

Hinckley's got all these contracts, but in order to fulfill them they needed to expand, buy machinery, and hire men. They tried to borrow money, but the bank wouldn't lend it to them, because the shops weren't worth the money that they needed to borrow. Tom Searls, of the First National Bank of Bar Harbor, and Ben Hinckley had to go to Boston, to the Federal Reserve Bank, and they got a stern lecture from some of those old bankers that this wasn't the way things were done.

But in the end they got the money, and they built the boats. Between Southwest Boat and Hinckley, I think they built something like 40 percent of the boats that came out of the state of Maine for the war effort.

During the first part of the war, a lot of fishing boats were taken for use by the Coast Guard. Then, as soon as new vessels were built for the Coast Guard, they'd send those boats back to their owners. Southwest Boat built quite a number of large draggers. They could get the material because it was a priority to build fishing boats to increase the nation's food supply. They also built a passenger boat for the Vinalhaven–Rockland ferry service and refitted a number of sardine boats. They once changed a sardine boat into a purse seiner during the war.

Manpower was scarce because all the young, able-bodied men were away in the service. So the yards hired a lot of older fellas who were house carpenters and laborers. They just put them to work building boats and tried to teach them what to do. But those men got an awful lot of work done. They didn't intend for these boats to last very long, and they weren't too fussy about how they were built, as long as they would do the job for a while.

As far as yachting went, things were pretty quiet during the war. People laid their boats up and left them because you couldn't get gasoline, and you were really restricted in where you could go in a boat anyway. The Coast Guard patrolled the harbor here all the time.

But fishermen didn't have to limit their travels too much. Fishing was encouraged because it was producing food for the national economy. But you had to have special numbers on your boat, and state registration numbers had to be painted in nine-inch letters. Then you had to put another big number on the top, so that the airplanes could read it. They had ration stamps for gasoline, but you could pretty much get gas for fishing.

Things were booming in the boatyards during the war, and they were full of workers. I was always going around to the shops, and I watched a lot of boats being built. It was great to see all that activity, and I learned quite a bit just by watching the men work. Sometimes it was easier to just look at what they were doing rather than ask any questions, because they wouldn't know how to tell you. And some builders wouldn't *want* to tell you anyway, so it was best to stand back and be quiet. If you just watched, you learned.

Lennox Sargent was a good draftsman and a pretty good designer. He had a nice drafting department at Southwest Boat during the war. There were quite a few people down there doing design work, and I would like to have seen their tools and how they did things. I was drawing boats at home and had to improvise my own equipment. As a matter of fact, I still do.

But I wish I had pushed my way into Southwest Boat. It might have helped as I went farther along in my own building. Of course, the work there was all restricted, and I was young—just sixteen in 1945. But if I'd pulled the strings right, I might have convinced my schoolteachers to get me in there.

In any event, by the time the war was over, the drafting business at Southwest Boat was a lot less. Sargent did it all himself, and there was not much for anyone else to do.

CHAPTER Eight

MY FATHER AND THE SUMMER PEOPLE

My father used to go fishing year-round, but he also worked for summer people. There's a long tradition of local fishermen doing that.

Summer people started to arrive on Mount Desert Island after the Civil War, in the 1870s mostly. The ones that came to Southwest Harbor at the time tended to be college professors, artists, ministers, schoolteachers, and people like that. They were highly educated for the most part and well-to-do enough so they could afford to come for the summer.

The summer people made quite a big change in the life around town. When they first came, they boarded in spare rooms in people's houses. All these local folks were good cooks, and the food was grown right here. They fed these summer people with the food that they ate themselves.

As more and more visitors came, hotels like the Island House and the Claremont sprang up. Some of the people that stayed there and boarded around town liked it so well that they bought land and had cottages built. They would bring their whole family and their servants and their horses and carriages. Some came here from Philadelphia, and many came here from New York and Boston. It must have been oppressive in the cities in those days because of the heat and the horses and the mud and dirt. So people came up to Maine.

They did a lot of boating and rowing, and the local people had what they needed. William Gilley had rowboats to rent, and some of the Gotts did, too. It was quite a big business in those days, and quite a few rowboats were built for that purpose.

Most of the summer people came by steamboat, but some of them had their own private yachts. The destination for most of the big yachts was Bar Harbor, but sometimes they'd stop in here at Southwest on the way. They also chartered local boats to go sailing in, and they had picnics and clambakes and went hiking. That was before Acadia National Park came into being, but there were trails and paths where they could go explore the mountains all over the island.

As the summer people got to know the area, word got around and more of their friends came. But they were generally the same kind of people. Over to Bar Harbor you got more of the wealthy type that built the mansions, and they were a cut above. But the people that came to Southwest Harbor seemed to fit in well and enjoyed the company of the local folks. Around here, people kind of mingled together.

In the old days, things weren't in such a hurry. The summer people would come, and you got to know them. You knew what to expect of them, and they knew what to expect of you. That relationship between the summer boarders and the local people was part of the character of the town. There might have been some differences, but most of the summer people wouldn't have been beneath coming to anybody's house and sitting down and having tea.

There's a story about a professor who used to come with his family to Islesford, on Little Cranberry Island. They built a big house, and then they bought a big field and wanted to put in a tennis court. They had it pretty near done, and their daughter was walking along there when one of the old fishermen came along. He made a remark about the tennis court and how they were building it.

"I hope," he says, "you don't play tennis here on Sunday."

She didn't know what to say, so she went home and told her father, "Mr. So-and-so said that he hoped that we didn't play tennis on Sunday."

"Well," her father says, "we *won't* play tennis on Sunday. This is their island. We're just visitors here, and if they don't want us to play tennis on Sunday, we won't."

That was the attitude of most of the summer people in those days. They were guests here, and I think if you went and knocked on their front door, you could come right in as a guest, too.

The local folks had something here that the summer people needed, and they were accepted as equals. Like sailing boats. The summer people looked up to the fishermen and respected them for their ability to sail and work on a boat.

That's how it was with my father and the Neilson family. He went to work for them some time in the early 1930s. They had been coming to Northeast Harbor from Pennsylvania for gener-

My father at the helm of the Leader *in 1935 or 1936.*

ations, and they were quite an influence on our lives. Mrs. Neilson, the grandmother, was an old lady when I was a boy. She was a Rosengarten, and that family had been coming to Northeast for years, too, probably since the late 1800s.

My father worked for the Neilsons for three months every summer, right through the Depression. In those days it worked out pretty good, because there was closed season on lobsters in the summer. Lobstering didn't start until the fall, so this summer work fitted right in.

He didn't sail them in his lobster boat. He used a boat called the *Leader* that Uncle Jimmy had had built, in 1926 I think it was. She was thirty-one feet, an open boat with a round spray

hood on the bow. She had a varnished deck and was nice looking and quite fast. Mrs. Neilson hired that boat for the summer from Uncle Jimmy and got my father to run it for her.

Her daughter Sarah had married a man named Madeira. Richie Stanley, who was my father's cousin, had been hired by the Madeiras, so he and my father pretty much worked for the same family. The Madeiras used Uncle Jimmy's boat, too, even though they had their own captain.

Mrs. Neilson's son Harry had three boys— Hank, Albie, and Benjie. Harry's wife died when Benjie was just a baby, and the boys were left with no mother. They did have a nanny, but my

*My father and mother at my sister Phoebe's
wedding in 1967.*

father had a lot to do with the care of those children in the summer. He had them out in the boat all the time. The Madeiras' son often went along with them, too. They thought a lot of my father, all of them.

His work in the summer often carried right into the night, because they'd go on picnics or parties after dark. As a matter of fact, he was over there most every night. Sometimes they'd go to Abel's Lobster Pound in the boat. At that time it was over in Mitchell's Cove, and they'd have to go around Bass Harbor Head to get to the lobster pound for their dinner. They'd come back late at night, and sometimes it would be thick o' fog.

One time when we had a babysitter and we were down at the steamboat wharf, my father came by in the *Leader* with Hank and Albie. He stopped and took us all on a little boat ride around the harbor. Hank and Albie were just little fellas, and they had their yachting uniforms on and their captain's caps. They were very formal and would shake hands.

Of course, that was in the early '30s. The old yachting traditions hadn't gone by the board at that time. The summer people dressed up, and my father had to have a uniform to sail them. The Neilsons sent him up to the Holmes Store in Northeast Harbor to get a captain's uniform with a cap and the whole works.

Mrs. Neilson also chartered a Friendship sloop called the *Reliance* from Jake Lunt, and my father sailed it for her. The *Reliance* was a thirty-six-footer that was built on Swans Island in the early 1900s. She had a make-and-break engine down in the cabin, and the propeller shaft went out through the side. Mrs. Neilson chartered that sloop during the war because gas was rationed, and she wanted to go out in something that wouldn't take much gasoline.

I can remember that old sloop. She was still good enough to sail in, but she had to be bailed every day. We'd go aboard of her, and there was a hatch in the floor where you could drop a bucket down in, like just dropping a bucket in a well. You'd pull out ten buckets every day, and she'd stay right even. You never got it all.

At that time—I was about twelve years old—my father used to go out trawling for hake before daylight when he'd get a chance. He'd be back in by nine o'clock, and then he'd be over to Northeast with the Neilsons for the rest of the day, and many times into the night. Since he was a fisherman, he could get gasoline for his boat, and if they had to go anywhere, they could go with him.

My father was off working most of the time, and he wasn't home much. He used to go out fishing by himself in those times, and I baited trawls for him. He'd unload the fish and leave the trawls at the dock. I spent that whole summer baiting trawls on the wharf, not only for my father but for other people, too. That was how I earned some money in those days.

When my father went trawling in the winter, he'd leave the house at about one o'clock in the morning. He might not get home until eleven o'clock that night, and sometimes he'd be out in some pretty tough weather. But there were a lot of boats trawling during the war, and they'd mostly be out there together.

I remember him bringing home the trawls and rigging them in the back room where we used to play. That tarred cotton line smelled some nice! He'd get a fire going in the wood-stove, and he'd put the hooks on those trawls in there. I think there were six hundred hooks on each line.

When I was a little older, I went fishing with him sometimes. Not an awful lot, though. We used to go out trawling and handlining. I'd bait the trawls in the boat, and he'd set them. The trawl had an anchor and floats on each end, and

Baker Island Light

the line in between laid on the bottom. You'd let it set for a long time and then haul it completely out and bait it and set it again. On the boat, I could bait a whole trawl in about half an hour, but on the dock it took an hour and a half. I don't know why.

At that time, we'd go trawling for haddock down off Baker's Island. Sometimes you'd get a whole bunch of them, and sometimes you'd get nothing. It varied quite a bit. We had a place where we'd set a trawl over a mussel bed. To find it, you had to get the lighthouse lined up just right against the mountains of Mount Desert Island.

Sometimes you'd get small halibut there, too,

and we got three or four one time. You could most always count on at least one. Sometimes, you'd get a mussel on the hook—one of these big red ones—and we'd save it for handline bait.

My father spent a lot of time on Baker's Island when he was growing up. At one time his mother, Mabel, had to take him and the other kids down there from Cranberry Island to stay with her people. Her husband, Arno Stanley, had some kind of a mental problem. He was strict with the kids and made them go out and earn money to buy things for the house.

When their old place on Cranberry Island was torn down, there were still barrels of flour that my father had earned money for and bought when he was ten or twelve years old. It wasn't a very good home life, so when Mabel got a chance they went somewhere better. My father lived with Uncle Jimmy for a while back on Cranberry.

One time, my father and his brother Robert decided to go off in a rowboat. Nobody knew where they'd headed, but one man said, "Well, they was rowing towards Baker's Island." Somebody telephoned down to the lighthouse and got the people there to watch for the two boys. Sure enough, they got down to Baker's Island all right. It was a nice place, and my father liked living out there.

Later, when I was about seventeen or eighteen, he took my sister Irene and me down to Baker's, and we walked all the way around the island on the shore. It was something he'd done when he was a boy and wanted to do again. So we did.

CHAPTER *Nine*

THE MILLIKENS, MRS. MONTGOMERY, AND MR. DUNN

Back in the early 1900s, there was a lady named Mrs. Gayley who came to Northeast Harbor with her two daughters, Agnes and Florence. She had a third daughter who was married and living in Italy, but I never met her at all. At that time, the two girls were teenagers, and I think Mrs. Gayley was a widow.

They stayed at the Harborside Inn, and Mrs. Gayley hired a captain. He turned out to be Charles Richardson, who went by the name Peter. He was my father's cousin, and he was a young man then. He had a little Friendship sloop, twenty-six feet long or something like that, and it was brand new. He had originally named her the *Alert,* but my Uncle Jimmy had a sloop by the

same name. So one of them had to be changed, and Peter changed his. At the last of it she was called the *Sweet Pea.*

Anyway, the girls came down one day and announced to their captain that they wanted to go to Blue Hill. Well, Peter figured he was there to do their bidding, so he didn't tell them how far Blue Hill was by water. It took them all day to get there, and it was late afternoon when they arrived. After they went to visit whoever it was they wanted to see, they started back to Northeast, and it took them a whole night to get there.

Naturally, Mrs. Gayley was frantic that her daughters were out there all alone with the captain. Somebody asked her who he was.

"Well, it's Peter Richardson," she said.

"Oh, don't worry about him. They'll be all right."

And they were.

Later on, when the girls married, they continued to come to Northeast in the summers. Agnes Gayley married Gerrish H. Milliken, who became the head of the Deering Milliken textile company. Mr. Milliken died in 1947, but he and Mrs. Milliken had two sons, named Gerrish and Roger, and two daughters. Their daughter Joan later became Mrs. Stroud, and their daughter Anne became Mrs. Franchetti.

Agnes's sister, Florence, who was called Folly, became Mrs. Montgomery. I never knew anything about Mr. Montgomery—he had died long before I came along—but he and Mrs. Montgomery had two daughters, Sylvia and Julia.

By the time I got to know the family, when I was about eighteen, Mrs. Gayley had married Mr. Gano Dunn. He was president of the J.G. White Engineering Corporation, in New York City, and he was a self-made man. He was real smart and an engineer, and he had worked his way up to become head of the company. They built airports over in Iran and Iraq and places like that back in the '40s and '50s.

Mr. Dunn used to come to Northeast Harbor summers, and it seems he had been sweet on Mrs. Montgomery before she was married. But he was a lot older than she was, and Folly would have nothing to do with him. He ended up marrying Mrs. Gayley, who was older than he was,

and so became Mrs. Montgomery's stepfather.

Originally, Mr. Dunn had a Bar Harbor S-boat, and he hired Harvey Stanley, my father's cousin on Cranberry Island, to sail him. They went down to Bristol, Rhode Island, and brought that boat up here. He had it for a number of years, and then he decided he wanted a bigger boat. So he had the schooner *Niliraga* built. She was an Alden-designed forty-three-foot centerboarder built by Goudy & Stevens in East Boothbay in 1928, and Harvey was captain of her until he died in 1941.

After Mr. Dunn married Mrs. Gayley, they lived on Sutton's Island in the summertime. They rented a house called the Little White Hen, and they used to keep the schooner out to Sutton's Island. Then after Mrs. Gayley died, Mr. Dunn brought the schooner into Northeast and had a mooring there, and he made his headquarters at the Millikens' when he came for the summer.

In 1947, I went to work for Mr. Dunn on that old schooner as cook and crew. I was eighteen and still in high school, and Neil Peterson was captain at that time. Mr. Dunn would stay aboard the schooner, but he'd go up to Mrs. Milliken's for dinner just about every night that we were in Northeast. When he'd come back to the dock, he'd blow his little whistle, and I'd have to be ready to row him back aboard. He couldn't see very well, and sometimes he'd blow his whistle when I was already right alongside of him.

I worked for him all that summer, and then I returned to high school in the fall. The next spring, we went to New York City on a class trip.

Niliraga *in 1941*

Everybody was going to a baseball game, but Allison Bunker and I didn't care about it, so he and I got permission from the teacher to go down to 80 Broad Street, where Mr. Dunn's office was. We called him up first, and he said, "Come right down!" We could have brought the whole class if they hadn't been going to the ball game.

We went on the subway and got to Broad Street and found the building and went upstairs. We told the receptionist who we were, and even though the office was full of people waiting to see Mr. Dunn, he took us right in. His office looked out over New York Harbor and the Statue of Liberty. I can't remember what floor it was on, but it was up quite high. At that time, Mr. Dunn was in his seventies. He showed us all around, and then he called in his right-hand man, Mr. McCabe, to take us on a special guided tour of NBC.

Mr. McCabe led us all around and showed us everything. We'd never seen television before, and they had the camera set up in one room and a TV set in another room. One of us stayed and watched the television while the other went in front of the camera. We could talk back and forth on the TV, and we got quite a kick out of that.

Then we went to see a radio show that was being broadcast. It was "Just Plain Bill," and here were these characters standing up in front of the microphones, reading the script. Of course, we were up in a soundproof room. We could look down and see them, and we could hear the voices, but the voices didn't fit the people at all. Here was this nice motherly voice, the woman speaking looked like somebody they'd dragged in off the street. Oh, she looked a mess. But here was this perfect voice coming out of the loudspeaker.

Then Mr. Dunn's assistant took us to the Automat and got us something to eat. Finally he put us on the subway back to the Times Square Hotel. On the way uptown, we were talking amongst ourselves about what station to get off at, and we thought, "We'll ask this guy."

We got talking with him, and he'd worked in New York all his life and was on his way home. We thought he'd be a good one to ask.

"Well, I don't know," he says. "I've never been up that far."

He'd lived in the city all his life, but he'd never been that far! We couldn't get over that.

CHAPTER *Ten*

LEAVING THE ISLAND FOR COLLEGE

I've lived in Southwest Harbor all my life, and I can't imagine going anywhere else to live or work. I suppose if I had to I would, but I've been able to do something right here and fit in where there was a need for building boats.

The most time I've ever spent away from Mount Desert Island was when I went to college up in Houlton. When I graduated from high school, I didn't know what I wanted to do, and here was this junior college that I could afford. I figured that would be a place to go until I could make a decision, and I had money enough to get through two years. When I started in 1948 it was called Ricker Junior College, but it became a four-year college the second year I was there. I stud-

ied liberal arts: English, geology, mathematics, calculus, history, psychology, and Spanish.

In those days, you could go up to Ellsworth and get a bus to Bangor and then take another bus to Houlton. Then other times, I used to go on the train after I got to Bangor. The first year they had the old-fashioned wooden passenger cars, and those had steam heat in them. The next year they had some brand-new cars. They were real nice—aluminum—and they rode a lot better. That was good, going on the train.

I stayed in the old dormitory up there. It was over a hundred years old at that time. It was the original 1848 classroom building of Ricker Classical Institute, and it had real high ceilings.

My room had great big windows, and it was on the northwest corner and was cold. It wasn't a very big room, and I had a fellow from Bucksport as a roommate.

In winter it'd get down to something like thirty-five below zero up there. The toilets flushed all the time and never stopped. The college had them on timers just to keep the water running. Otherwise they'd have frozen up quicker than a wink. If you went down to the bathroom to wash up and wet your hair down to comb it, by the time you got back to your room your hair would be frozen.

The wind would blow right through that place, but we had our room fixed up pretty good after I got hold of some heavy brown paper. We pulled down the shade curtains on the windows, and put this big brown paper over them and taped it right down tight.

Just before we closed up the top, we filled the cavity full of balled-up newspapers to make insulation and crammed them in there and sealed it right up. That warmed up the room quite a bit. I had more of that brown paper, and I put it on my bed, too! Pretty good insulation, that stuff. Of course it didn't let in any light through the windows, but it didn't let in so much cold, either.

One night the heat went out. The students weren't supposed to have electric heaters, but we had one, and there were something like twenty-one people in my room, including three or four teachers. We had the heater going, and they never said a word about it!

I'd go down to the town library in Houlton quite often. I could take books out, but many times I'd stay right there because it was nice and warm. It wasn't long before I had the run of the place. I could go anywhere in the stacks, so I used to hunt around for books—not only about boatbuilding, but also about history.

I read a lot while I was there at college. I've always had an interest in history, especially local history, and I discovered Sprague's *Journals of Maine History* and read those through and through. I also found Howard Chappelle's books on boat design and boatbuilding, and I used to study them. I had a drawing board in my room, and I designed boats then, too.

One of the courses I enjoyed was Spanish. I got straight A's right through, and it was easy. I hardly had to think about it. It came right to me. Most of it was writing and reading. We didn't do much with the spoken language.

In the second year, we had a new teacher who was right out of Bates College. When she came through the door for the first class, she was talking Spanish. Everybody was looking around and thinking, "What's she talking about?"

I couldn't get a word of it at first, but I thought, "I'll listen sharp, and maybe I'll catch something." The last thing she said was something about "los libros." Well, that means "the books," and I thought, "She's talking about books." (On the bulletin board, there'd been a notice about books we were supposed to have.)

That teacher looked around the whole class to get an answer from somebody. All the students were looking dumbfounded, but when she looked

The lobster-style powerboat Cinchona, *which I built for Hank Neilson in 1993, was named after the family's yawl.*

my way, I just held up my book and smiled. Sure enough, that's what it was! I was off to a good start.

If I had gone through a full four years of college, I would like to have studied languages. About that time the United Nations was starting up, and I thought, "Wouldn't it be nice to understand a lot of languages, to go there and work." I didn't particularly like New York City, but I thought it would be a great opportunity to do something like that.

During the summers of 1948 and 1949, I came home from college and worked on the Neilsons' boat with my father. She was a forty-four-foot Casey yawl called the *Cinchona*. My father had to go on some cruises with them to Nova Scotia, and one time they went down to the

Harvard–Yale rowboat race in New London. I went as far as Manchester, Massachusetts, on that trip and came back on a train.

Whenever I got home from college on vacation, I always made a trip to the boatyards around the island to see what was going on there. Raymond Bunker was closest, and I used to visit him quite often. Cliff Rich and his sons Robert, Ronald, and Roger were all building boats at that time, too.

Cliff had a little shop in back of his house over in Bernard, and Robert was down on the shore. Ronald was there, too, until he got out on his own and came over here to Southwest. He rented Roger's boatshop and built boats there for a while, then later on he built his own shop on the Herrick Road, next to his house.

HOW I BUILT MY FIRST BOAT

When I went away to college, I didn't have any idea of what I wanted to do for a living, but I knew that I did want to build a boat at some point. I graduated in 1950 with an associate's degree in liberal arts, and I didn't have money enough to go to school for another year. So I thought, "Well, I'll work this summer and earn enough money to start a boat."

All I needed was something like $150 to buy materials for a twenty-eight-foot lobster boat. So I came home and got a job that summer working for the Millikens. My great-uncle Lew Stanley was sailing them, and he was getting pretty old. Mrs. Milliken had told him the year before that she was going to find somebody to help him. So I applied

for the job. They talked it over with Mr. Dunn, and at first they decided they didn't need anybody. Uncle Lew could do it all right.

When the Millikens came for the summer, they wanted Uncle Lew to bring the motor launch up to take some of them fishing. As it happened, he was sick and couldn't do it. So he asked me if I would sail the boat over and take them out fishing, and I did. Then they wanted to go again. At that time I was also working down at Cranberry Island for Uncle Lew's son Boynton, getting the boats down there ready for summer. So I took the boat up to Northeast and took them fishing again.

Then they called me to come and see Mrs. Milliken one morning at nine o'clock. I went over

Lew and me with the Niliraga *at dockside, about 1952.*

to the house and talked with her, and they hired me to help Uncle Lew on the boat. They had an old twenty-eight-foot open launch that I sailed them in, and I earned enough money to buy some materials that fall and start my own boat.

Boatbuilding was beginning to pick up again by this time. Southwest Boat was turning out some big commercial vessels, and Henry Hinckley was building mostly sailboats, but it was a hard job to sell his wooden boats. He swutched to fiberglass some time in the '50s, and that saved him.

There were still quite a few smaller builders in the area then. Sim Davis had a shop on the McKinley side of Bass Harbor, and I used to visit him now and then. He was building workboats mostly. Farnham Butler built boats, too, but I didn't get there much. That was way up in Somesville, and I hardly ever got beyond Carroll's Hill. I still don't.

Norman Bouchard also built boats about that time. He had come to town with the CCC and had married a local girl. He got a job in the boatyard during the war, and he picked up how to build boats. After the war boom was done, he started building on his own, and he turned out some fairly good ones. They were mostly lobster boats, but there were some pleasure boats, too.

I also remember a fella named Philips Lord, who started a boat shop up in Somesville, in the barn of the old Somes House. He got a fella named Gaudette from Nova Scotia to come down and help him. They didn't last very long in business, maybe two years, but they got all these boats to build. They were big ones, but none of them were awfully pretty.

One time, they had this party boat to build, and it needed to have a toilet in it. They thought, "Gee whiz, there's no need to buy a toilet to put in there. We'll just run an eight-inch pipe right up through the hull and build it right in there and just put a cover over it. It'll be fine." So they did that, and they put the boat off. When they started running her wide open, there was an eight-inch head of water coming up out of the pipe! So they had to change that.

Then there was Les Rice, who had started building boats on Sutton's Island. Later he moved over to Cranberry Island and set up a shop there. During the war he came up here and worked at Southwest Boat.

With everybody that was building boats, I used to look their work over, compare their models, and compare their methods. Some things I liked about their boats, and some things I didn't. I always tried to take the best out of all of them and put it into my own models.

Of all the builders, Raymond Bunker probably had the strongest influence on me. As a matter of fact, I'm related to him, and I'd known him since I was a boy. Raymond was from Cranberry Island, and he built boats over there before he came up here. In those days, that was like another world. It still is.

Here I am, dressed for work on the schooner.

Cranberry was a hard place to build a boat. Everything had to be brought over to the island before you could start in. Raymond said they had an oak keel delivered over to the steamboat wharf at Clark Point one time back in the early '30s, and they came up in a boat to get it. It was setting on the wharf, and they said, "Well, we'll just throw it overboard and tow it back down."

So they pushed the keel into the water, and it went right to the bottom. They managed to get hold of one end of it and tow it across. Then they had to drag it up the beach and wrassle it onto a truck to get it down to the shop.

Raymond had worked with Chester Clement at the boatyard, and he learned a lot from Chester. Raymond was helpful to me like that.

I never worked as a carpenter in any of the shops. After college, I just came back and started on my own. I didn't have very many tools to begin with, just the essentials and that was it. I had a

No. 3 jack plane, and that's not really a good tool to get out long planks with. I think I used six C-clamps on the first boat I built, and I've still got them, but that's all I had then. Now we've got a whole wall full, and we seem to use them all. But you could build a boat without too many tools, really.

I still have some tools that I acquired when I was getting started. I've got a Skil electric plane that I bought in 1957. It needs to be repaired, but it's still usable. I bought three other ones after that, but none of them stood up like the first one.

If I were in that situation today—trying to start a boatbuilding business—the neighbors would have a fit. But things were different when I got started. People encouraged me. George Higgins lent me an adze, and different ones lent me other tools and helped me with things that I needed.

George Noyes brought up a long jointer plane for me to use. He was an interesting fella, really

Raymond Bunker (foreground) with his partner, Ralph Ellis, getting out a plank on a bandsaw in 1976.

Raymond and Ralph planking up a boat at their shop in Manset in 1976.

enthusiastic and interested in all kinds of things. He was a roller skater, and he also pitched horseshoes. He won the horseshoe championship one time somewhere in Maine.

He worked down at Hinckley's during the war, and after it ended they were making paddles there. They had these drums to sand the paddles on, and the place was awfully dusty. So George made himself a respirator. He put some gauze over the top of a pepper shaker that he could put in his mouth and breathe through. It was quite an ingenious invention, and it worked. After that, Hinckley started looking into regular respirators, manufactured ones.

Anyway, I got some lumber, and I had the use of my grandfather's paint shop out back of my grandmother's house, where my mother and father and grandmother and I all lived. I set up the boat that fall and planked her up that winter.

That twenty-eight-foot lobster boat was my own design. I made a half model and took the lines off of it to make the full-size molds. I pretty much knew how to do that, and I didn't have to think about it much. It just seemed to come to me. When I started building and I'd get stuck on something, I'd go around to boat shops on the island and see how they'd done it. Then I'd go back and figure out what I could do. I learned as I went along.

The next summer I worked some more for Mrs. Milliken and earned enough money to make a down payment on an engine and buy some more

My first boat, tied up at the lower town dock in Southwest Harbor in 1952.

materials to get the boat finished. I finally got her launched on May 1, 1952.

At the time, I didn't think I'd end up building boats for a living. But a couple of months later, along came Dick Yates and wanted me to build him a boat. I couldn't wait to get started. And people have been after me to build boats for them ever since.

I had my twenty-eight-footer for a few years, but I never named her. I used her to go back and forth to Uncle Lew's boatyard on Cranberry Island. I was working on a boat that was stored down there, one that Raymond Bunker had built for the Millikens.

Fishing appealed to me, but I never did much of it. I used to get out with my father some, but I wasn't very strong when I was younger, and you've got to be strong to be a fisherman.

I used my boat a little bit for handlining, and I had a good time. I didn't make any great amount of money with it, but it was fun to do. Back then you could dig clams for bait up in Norwood's Cove, and sometimes I'd go in to the mill dam, where the tide comes out through, and I'd gather up those big red mussels for bait.

I'd take my boat up and anchor right there off the shore and row in and dig clams and mussels. Then I'd go out handlining. Sometimes I took people with me, and sometimes I went alone. But I never really thought much about fishing for a living.

I had my first boat about three years, until I got sick. When that happened, I sold her to Charlie Gilley. He went lobstering winters and sailed Mrs. Lyman from Sutton's Island in that boat during the summer. He used that twenty-eight-footer as a workboat to take her in to Northeast Harbor and carry groceries back to the island and do whatever needed to be done out there.

I can't remember whether his job ended or whether Mrs. Lyman just got so old she didn't come to Sutton's Island any more. Anyway, he laid the boat up for a while, and then he sold her. The last I saw of my boat, she was over to Marlboro, on the beach in a cradle. I was told later that somebody was taking her down east and they got her on a ledge and she smashed to pieces. But I don't know for sure. I haven't seen her since.

CHAPTER *Twelve*

MY WORK IS INTERRUPTED

In the summer of 1953, I was working for the Milliken family in Northeast Harbor. I was tired, all in, and couldn't figure out what was wrong. They couldn't seem to find the answer here in Southwest Harbor, so in the fall, I went to Bangor, and a doctor examined me up there.

He said I had one of three things—either cancer, tuberculosis, or a lung abscess. He thought probably it was a lung abscess, but before they could figure out what was really wrong, I had to go to Boston. They turned me inside out and found out for sure.

Actually, I had both an abscess and tuberculosis in the right lower lobe of my lung. I'd had a tooth pulled out and got the abscess from

that. Then the tuberculosis snuck in there somehow and took over.

In those days, if you had tuberculosis you went to a sanatorium and took streptomycin shots twice a week and had to rest in bed. After the tuberculosis germ became inactive, they'd operate to take out that part of the lung. Then you went and spent more time in the sanatorium after the operation. Today they don't do that.

So, first I went to the sanatorium in Bangor. There was only one other fella besides me there at the hospital. The girls were upstairs. It was pretty lonesome, a lonely place. I didn't particularly like it there, but I stuck it out for six months and got my weight up from a hundred and thirty pounds to one-eighty.

Then I went to Boston and had the lower right lobe of the lung removed. I was operated on April 5, 1954. That's a date that sticks in my mind like December 7, 1941—Pearl Harbor. I was in Boston three weeks for the operation, and then I came back to Fairfield Sanatorium in Maine for the recuperation. I got up to a hundred and ninety pounds there, and in the fall of 1954 they discharged me.

I was laid up just about a year. But I was better than ever after the operation. For years and years afterwards I was not sick at all, and I was stronger than I'd ever been.

When I first came home from the sanatorium, I wasn't supposed to do much. That winter, I helped Raleigh Stanwood build a little outboard boat, and I also worked on Great Cranberry Island, at Uncle Lew's old boatyard, which his son Boynton ran for him.

After Boynton gave it up, Steve Spurling and I took over the yard and ran it for a couple of years, doing maintenance. He's a cousin to me, too, my father's sister's son. Steve was older than I was, so I didn't get to know him until after he got out of the service. Anyway, that really didn't work out, so we gave it up.

About that time, one of my sisters was friends with Marion Linscott. She was born over in Hancock, and I remember when she was a little girl just coming to town here, in 1935 or 1936. The family came in a boat that her father, Henry, and his brother-in-law owned. She was

named the *Edna C*, and she was an old lobster smack. They had repaired her over to Lamoine, and Henry came down here and lived aboard of her for a while and worked in the sardine factory.

When it got to be cold weather, the Linscotts all moved up into one of the factory camps. They found that was full of bedbugs, so they switched into another one. They lived in those camps for several years and then rented other places around town. Finally, Henry bought a house down the road here. Next, he rented out that place and bought another house up the road, and that's where they were living when Marion and I got serious.

I was friends with Charlie Gilley, and Marion was working as a babysitter for him and his wife Christine. Carlton Gilley and Walter Lewis and some other fellas were talking about making a date with Marion, but they never did. So I decided I would. We went to a basketball game, and we started going around together. Marion's whole family went to Florida that winter, and when they got back we resumed dating. That fall we got married.

For our honeymoon, we went for a three-day cruise on the *Niliraga*. We stopped first at Burnt Coat Harbor on Swan's Island, and the next day we continued up to Camden. We went as far as Pulpit Harbor on North Haven and then came home.

It wasn't until the wedding that I finally moved out of my grandmother's house. Marion and I rented an apartment in Southwest for $35 a month. We were there for about a year when

Marion and me on our wedding day in 1956.

Above: Richard, Edward, Nadine, Marjorie, Marion, and me on a family outing to Georges' Pond in Franklin in 1967. Left: Nadine, Marjorie, Richard and Edward at Easter (about 1968).

our daughter Nadine was born in June 1957. But the landlady didn't want babies in the house, so the next winter we rented Albie Neilson's house down to Seawall. That was a great big place, and back then he wanted to keep it heated for the winter and wanted somebody in it.

When we moved out of Albie's in the spring, we rented a little house down off Clark Point Road. It had four rooms and a hall. That place was $35 a month, too. The hall went the whole length of the thing, with two rooms on each side. There was a door on each end, and the wind would blow right through it.

Oscar Krantz's twenty-eight-footer tied up alongside the Stanley fish wharf in Manset,
where I used to bait trawls as a boy.

Then in April of 1959, we moved into the house where we live now on Clark Point Road, and our daughter Marjorie was born in June of that year. At that time my father owned the house, and we rented from him. He had inherited it from Uncle Jimmy. Years later, after my father died, I inherited it.

When Uncle Jimmy first moved off Cranberry Island, he had rented over in Manset for a time. Then about 1928 he had this house built. His wife, Aunt Nan, thought that he should be near a doctor because she thought that he had a bad heart, but then she died first, right here in this house, in 1933. After that Uncle Jimmy's niece, Mrs. Fletcher, came and kept house for him. She died here, too, and then he didn't have anybody.

He stayed here alone, but my father and mother would come in and help out. Along to the last of it he got kind of demented. He used to see people talking to him. He'd be sitting here in his rocking chair, and all of a sudden he'd holler, "Get out of here! Get out of here!"

My father would come out and say, "Nobody here."

"Yes, there is, too," Uncle Jimmy would argue. "They're here bothering me. Get 'em out of here."

My father couldn't do a thing with him. So my mother would come out and take the broom and shoo out the imaginary people.

"There," she'd say. "They're gone now."

And Uncle Jimmy would say, "Yup, but they'll come back."

Anyway, he was about ninety-six when he died, and he had outlived Aunt Nan by twenty years or so. They never had any children of their own, but a lot of children lived with them. My father did when he was young, and my Aunt Esther did, too. They were always taking in some young person. So I knew the house when I was growing up. It wasn't that far from my grandmother's place, and I can remember coming here and visiting, both with Aunt Nan before she died and when Mrs. Fletcher lived here.

When Marion and I got married I had to do something to make a living. I didn't have a boat to build right then, and Lennox Sargent wanted me to get a job down at Southwest Boat. I gave it some serious thought, and I was all set to do it when Oscar Krantz came by at the last minute and wanted a lobster boat. I said "Okay, I'll build her." I was quite relieved to have a boat to work on that winter. That was a twenty-eight-footer that we launched in the spring of 1957.

At that time I was still working for a good part of the year on the *Niliraga* out of Northeast Harbor. Mr. Dunn had died, and Mrs. Montgomery had inherited the schooner. She didn't use it for a couple of years, and she had a couple of captains that really didn't prove out. Then they put me on the schooner, and I was her captain for 19 years, until 1974.

In my early years as a boatbuilder, I'd work summers on the schooner and sail her from July to October. In the spring I got her ready. In the fall, I laid her up. It made about nine months work. Around 1958, after I moved to Clark Point Road, I built a track behind the house and started hauling her up and storing her right here. Then

I'd build either one or two boats during the winter. The work overlapped in the spring and the fall.

Mrs. Montgomery never really learned how to sail. When she'd steer, the wake would be all crooked, and she didn't know when to come about. We were out sailing one day, and her niece, Mrs. Stroud's daughter, was there. Mrs. Montgomery and I had it worked out that when it was time to come about, I'd go down to the leeward side and take hold of the jib sheet. When I did that, she'd say, "Ready about. Hard alee." And we'd come about.

Mrs. Stroud's daughter was watching these proceedings, and she says, "Aunt Folly, how is it that Ralph knows every time you want to come about?"

"Well," says Mrs. Montgomery in a gruff voice, "Ralph and I have sailed together for a good many years. He knows what I'm going to do."

But she did get so she liked sailing after a while, and we did a lot of it. "It's a funny thing," she'd say. "When Mr. Dunn was alive, he used to ask me to go out sailing, and I hated it. I dreaded it, but I had to go. Now here I am doing the same thing myself. I'm asking people to go out sailing with me."

Sometimes she and I would be out on that schooner all alone in October, and it was nice. She'd get me telling stories about the history of the place, and she'd say, "Ralph, you must write this down. You be sure and write this down."

CHAPTER *Thirteen*

I ENJOYED BUILDING WORKBOATS

During the early years, I worked pretty much by myself, but sometimes I'd get someone to help me. When I built my own boat—that first twenty-eight-footer—I was all alone, and it took me two winters. Then when I got the boat for Dick Yates, I designed it and lofted it out and made the molds. I asked Millard Spurling to come up and help me build it.

Millard was quite an old man at that time, in his seventies I'd guess. I got the boat started, and then he came up. We had the boat set up and maybe timbered out when he got sick and had to stop work. So I carried on alone, but Millard came back in the spring and helped me do some of the finishing.

The next boat I built was a twenty-eight-footer for Roland Sprague down to Islesford, on Cranberry Island, and we launched her in 1958. Fred Black helped me with that boat and for a while after that. He was related to me through the Robinsons, some kind of a cousin.

That same winter I also built a boat for a man named Merritt Bean in New Hampshire. He was some relation of L.L. Bean, and he owned property down in Casco Bay. He planned to use the boat down there. Fred Black and I worked together on those two projects that winter, and then he went on to other things. That boat we built for Merritt Bean was interesting. He was going to bring us a rebuilt automobile engine to

Merritt Bean's Volkswagen-powered boat ready to launch.

use. We had already put the beds in for the engine when he landed in front of the shop one day and says, "I've got the engine out on a trailer."

I said, "How are we going to get it in here?"

"Oh, I think we can lug it in," he says. "There's been a little change."

On the trailer was this little Volkswagen engine. We lugged it in all right, four of us. It was air-cooled, and we had to put a thrust bearing on the shaft and have a double universal made. We ended up putting some engine beds on top of the cabin floor, and then we fastened the engine right down. But it worked fine.

There were two four-inch aluminum pipes that served as the support for the back of the steering shelter and that housed the exhaust pipes. The actual exhausts were two three-quarter-inch tubes that went through the middle of those big pipes. There were no mufflers, and when you'd start the engine and open her up quick, it sounded like a package of firecrackers going off. Merritt had that engine in the boat for quite a while, but finally he put a Mercedes diesel in it.

The next winter, I built a workboat for a Mrs. O'Brien over to Seal Harbor. That was also the winter that Roland Sprague was lost in his boat. He and Fred Fernald went out lobstering in March of 1959, and they never came back. A tough snowstorm came up, and they didn't make it.

We had put a Chevrolet engine in Roland's boat when we built her, but he had just switched to a new Palmer that burned a lot more gas than the old Chevrolet. The theory was that he and Fred ran out of gas outside of Baker's Island somewhere, and they drifted in across the Bass Harbor bar. Their boat was found the next day, on

My father's boat, the Seven Girls, being towed to her launching.

Pond Island up in Blue Hill Bay. Both of them were in the cabin, and of course they were dead. They died from exposure, I guess. It was a hard job to get back to work after that, but I did. Even though it wasn't my fault, they were lost in my boat. But it survived and was used for a good many years afterwards. Finally it was sold down to Swans Island, and I don't know whether it's gone to pieces yet or not.

Then in 1960, I built a boat for my father. He'd had two workboats before. The one he was out all night in that time back in 1935 was a little double-ender, built on Cranberry Island. Then he bought a bigger boat—the thirty-four-footer that Chester Clement had built for Harvard Beal. But that old boat was getting pretty ratty, so the Neilsons wanted to have a new one built for him, and they came to me. At the time, I was living down here on Clark Point Road. This was still my father's house, and I was renting it from him. The rent was going

towards the house—which I was going to get anyway—and I hauled boats up in back, too.

My father wasn't a boatbuilder, but he probably could have been if he'd had to. He had a pretty good idea of how things were put together. We got along okay. I helped him sometimes with repairs on his boat, and he helped me from time to time in the shop.

We talked about what he'd like to have in the boat. At first, we were going to make the boat thirty-two feet long, but his other one was thirty-three feet nine inches. So we built it thirty-three. I made a half model of it, and he approved of that. He worked on the new boat with me some when I was building it, but I did it mostly alone.

He named her the *Seven Girls* for my seven sisters, his seven daughters. He used her for lobstering and sometimes for scalloping. He used her to sail the summer people, too. He had that boat for ten years. When my father died in 1971,

"Tommy" Spurling's thirty-three-footer, the Rachel Ann, *was built on the same model as the* Seven Girls.

she was sold out of the family, and she had three or four other owners after that. The last one had the boat out here in Southwest Harbor, off the town dock, and she got run into. I went out and saved her from sinking and the owner sold the damaged boat to me. I repaired her, and I've still got her.

After the *Seven Girls*, I built twenty-some motorboats that were either lobster boats, workboats, or pleasure boats. They ranged in length from twenty-six to forty-four feet.

In 1961, I built a boat for Emerson Spurling Sr. It was just like the *Seven Girls*, on the same model, except the cabin wasn't so long. He and his son owned it together. Emerson Jr. worked with me on the building of it, and altogether he helped me with twelve boats, I think it was.

Then we built him a boat that we finished in 1968, and after that he went lobstering. But he was a big help in those years.

Emerson Sr. used to be called Tommy, and he used his boat for lobstering and for trawling. I remember that they brought in the biggest catch of haddock, moneywise, that had ever come to the Manset fish wharf up to that time. They had something like $575 in one day's trip. That was a good catch in the early '60s. Lawrence Newman was out there and came in first with $375 worth, but Tommy was still hauling. He said to Lawrence, "For God's sakes, don't tell them on the fish wharf how many I've got. They'll stop buying before I get in." Tommy had that boat for quite a while.

In 1965, I came out with a new design. For

Launching Russell Pettigrove's lobster boat.

that one, I didn't make a half model. I just drew it out on paper. It was thirty-four feet long and was built for Wendell Seavey. He went trawling for hake in the summer, and he also went hand-lining in the spring and the summer, when the pollack were schooling.

Wendell once brought in a load of fifteen thousand pounds of pollack in that boat, and her name on the transom wasn't even under-water. She held up real good, held a lot of weight. They were catching them on these bait-ed balloons, shaped like a little worm, and they had seven hooks on a line. They'd haul in seven pollack to a time. Oh, their hands were all raw.

Wendell had that boat for a number of years. Then he got out of fishing and sold her down to South Bristol somewhere. I think she's still there. The next winter I built one just like

Wendell's for Russell Pettigrove, and I used that model quite a few times afterwards.

One time, Russell was coming in from Duck Island and there was a fiberglass boat alongside of him. The guy in the fiberglass boat was steer-ing her to beat the band, and she'd yaw this way and yaw that way, just thrashing around and rolling. But Russell would let go of the wheel and his boat would ride the sea and just keep going straight. He had his teacup on his bulk-head, and it wasn't even upset.

I didn't have much of a building crew in those days. It might be me and another man, like Emerson Jr. or Steve Spurling. Usually there was just two or three of us. It wasn't full-time employment because these fellas did other things, but I was set up to pay them wages when they worked. In the springtime, we'd have a few

Jarvis Newman at his shop in Manset in 1975.

more people, including a few older fellas that were around.

Steve started working with me about 1965 and, as I say, he worked with me quite a few years. He was a big help in building the boats. He'd worked at Southwest Boat, and he knew quite a lot about how things should be done.

In 1971, I didn't have a boat to build myself, so I went over to Jarvis Newman's and worked for him, on an old Friendship sloop called the *Venture*. I can remember Jarvis as a kid being around the dock in the summer when the boats would come in with fish. At the time, his family was living in Connecticut, and his father, Lawrence, would come home and go haking for

a couple of weeks with his own father, Lyle.

Later on, when Jarvis's father retired from his work in Connecticut, they came back here to work and live year-round. I didn't know Jarvis much, but I remember him working summers in the Gordon and White garage during high school. Then he went away to school. He married Raymond Bunker's daughter, Susan, and they lived away for a time.

When she and Jarvis came back to Southwest, he went to work for Hinckley, and about that time he was starting to mold fiberglass rowboats. He used to come into my shop and look things over. Later on, he went into business for himself and was building fiberglass lobster boats and Friendship sloops. He'd make the molds using old wooden boats for the plugs, and he also did repair work.

Originally, Jarvis had engaged his father-in-law, Raymond Bunker, to help rebuild the *Venture*. Raymond didn't have a boat to build that year, and it was around the first of November that the appointed day came. Jarvis had the boat in the shop, all cleaned out, and Raymond was supposed to come in that morning and go to work on her. Well, Raymond showed up, but he didn't bring any tools or anything. He just came in and stood up against the bench and chewed on his pipe a little bit. Then he says, "Gosh, Jarvis, I can't work on that rotten old thing." And out he went.

That night, Jarvis came over to my house and asked me to help him. I said, "Well, yeah, I'll come down and do what I can, but if I get a boat to build, I'll have to stop."

About the last of December in 1970, I had the *Venture* mostly done when in came James Robbins and wanted me to build him a thirty-three-foot lobster boat. I said sure and told Jarvis I had to leave. He took over the Friendship sloop from there, and I went over nights and weekends afterwards and put on the trailboards and things like that for him.

Steve Spurling and I started the Robbins boat around the first of January. Then I found out that James was a boatbuilder and that he'd turned out four or five boats himself. I thought, "Oh, gosh. What have I got myself into? He's a boatbuilder and he'd do things differently than I do and we'll be at odds all the time. I'll just have to make the best of it."

Well, I started building the boat. James came over, not saying a thing, and it turned out he was one of the easiest fellas to build for. It was no problem at all. I'd save up things and ask him, like, "How do you want to do this?" and "How do you want to do that?" He'd just say, "You're building the boat. Do it the way you want to."

So, I did, and after I got her done, he came and got her. They towed her to Stonington and put the engine in down there. Afterwards he wrote me a letter saying he'd never had anything in his life that he was more satisfied with. I thought it turned out good, too, and he was still using her into his 80s. In the spring of 2000 he sold her, but she's still in use.

In the 1970s, I did make one model especially for Jarvis Newman. Using that, we built a thirty-two-foot lobster boat out of wood for one of the local fishermen with the understanding that Jarvis could take a mold off of it for the Newman 32. Then I would get royalties from some of the fiberglass boats Jarvis built.

There's one of those Newman 32s over to the Hawaiian Islands. The owner came to Maine one time and was telling me about that boat. He said he could go out there in those great big Pacific swells when the other boats were high-tailing it for home, and they didn't bother him a bit. The weather can get quite rough out there. It breezes up with big swells. But he said that boat took it fine.

The pleasure boats I've built are pretty much based on lobster-boat hulls. I haven't really departed from that too much, unless I know that the owner's going to put a lot of stuff in them. Then I make them a little fuller and build them a little different than I would a lobster boat.

I've always liked to build fishing boats. That's what I did first and for the next ten years, pretty much. There were a couple of pleasure boats in between, but they were plain, more like fishing boats and nothing fancy. They were all my own designs. I didn't take anybody else's plan or shape.

The work got quite steady. Sometimes I had as many as three boats ahead of me. I built twenty-seven in the old shop, and I don't know how we worked in there and turned out as many boats as we did, because it was so cold. It was nothing more than an old barn, and it just sat on the ground, with no foundation or anything. Some mornings it would be down to zero or below, and by quitting time it might still be only thirty-five degrees.

Generally, there's not much call for wooden lobster boats any more. It costs so much to build them. I don't think the banks encourage financing a wooden lobster boat. The insurance companies don't favor wood, either. I don't know why not, because I've got some boats that are thirty years old, and there are no problems with the hulls themselves.

It depends on maintenance. Wooden lobster boats that are out there working all the time and are covered with salt water don't have near the problems of a boat that's laid up. The worst problem is in the top of the boat, where fresh water gets down in the deck and around the seams, causing rot.

Today, the decks can be fiberglassed or epoxied and made watertight. But even that has to be taken care of. If you've got a leak, you need to fix it right quick. If anybody lets a wooden boat sit, it will go downhill fast, but most of the fellas that I built for have taken pretty good care of their boats.

It was fun to build those boats because they were out working, and they were doing something productive. They were contributing to the economy and the life of the community.

CHAPTER *Fourteen*

MY FIRST FRIENDSHIP SLOOP

I always liked the look of Friendship sloops. They just caught my eye. I think that Friendships caught Albie Neilson, too. His grandmother had once chartered the *Reliance*, which my father had sailed her on. In the late '50s, Albie told me that someday he wanted me to build him a Friendship sloop, so I took more interest in them then.

In 1961, the first Friendship sloop regatta was held in Friendship, Maine. When I read about that in the paper, I told Mrs. Montgomery that there was going to be a race down there. Her first recollections of sailing around here were in a Friendship sloop, and that was the experience of many of the summer people back then.

"Well, let's go," she said.

So we went down in the schooner with her niece and Emerson Spurling, who helped me build boats in the winter. That first regatta only lasted one day, and sixteen or seventeen boats took part. I'd never seen so many Friendships together at one time, and I thought that was something. It had been quite a while since I'd seen one sailing, and it gave me a good chance to look them over, get some ideas, and refresh my memory.

When Albie was ready to have his boat, I built him a thirty-three-footer called *Hieronymus*. She was the first Friendship sloop and the first sailboat that I ever built. I started her in 1961, and we launched her in 1962. My father-in-law, Henry Linscott, worked on the interior and helped in the

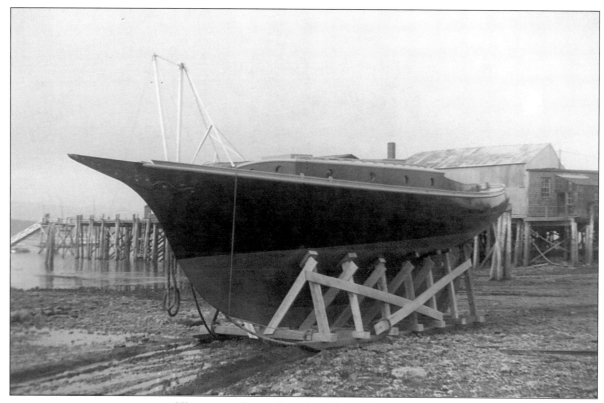

Hieronymus *in cradle, prior to launching in 1962.*

Richard and Edward

finishing off of that boat. It took more than a winter to get it completed. That March our son Richard was born, and we put the boat in the water in June.

After *Hieronymus,* I had plenty of work building lobster boats and I didn't turn out any more sloops for a while. During the winter of 1962–63, I built two boats, a twenty-six-foot lobster boat for a summer person and a twenty-eight-foot boat for a lobsterman. In the fall of 1963, I started to build a thirty-two-foot lobster boat for Carroll Chapin of Isle au Haut. My father-in-law, Henry Linscott, worked with me on all three of those boats. Our son Edward was born on November 15, 1963, and this was about the time we started to build the Chapin boat.

Hieronymus *on her maiden voyage.*

There's been a lot written about the origin of the Friendship sloops and what they are, but Wilbur Morse was asked one time what a Friendship sloop was. He said it was a sloop built in Friendship by Wilbur Morse, and he was right. Some people would dispute that, even though he probably built the most sloops of anybody. Others would say that the only real Friendships were the ones built by the McLains and that Morse stole their model.

Wilbur Morse and the McLain family were the most prominent of the original builders who were active before 1915 or 1920. But there was also Albion Morse in Cushing. He was the builder of the *Morning Star.* And then there was Jonah

Morse, Wilbur's brother, who worked with him in Friendship.

Another of Wilbur's brothers, Charles Morse, had his own shop at Hatchet Cove in Friendship. He later built sloops in Thomaston. There's a boat named the *Vigor* that is still sailing, and she was built by Charles Morse. Another one of his boats was the *Alice Marion.* She was a thirty-six-foot round-bow sloop, and she was at Cranberry Island. My father's cousin, Richie Stanley, owned that boat and used her to go fishing.

She carried a crew of three—Richie Stanley, Ernest Stanley, and Charles Stanley—and they'd go off for three or four days, towing a dory to haul their trawls in. They'd be out of sight of land and thirty or forty miles at sea. They'd set the trawls from the sloop and haul them into the dory while one fella tended the boat. They'd fish until they got a load and then sail home.

On the way in, they'd set the tiller and go down below and play cards and let her sail herself. The tiller had a comb that it dropped into, so that it would stay in one place. They'd get the sails trimmed right and let her go. Every now and then they'd look out to see if they were headed right.

The original Friendship sloops were all built to serve the purpose of fishing and lobstering. Most of these boats were built in the twenty-five- to twenty-eight-foot range, although they might be up to almost fifty feet in length. They had a cabin up off the deck, and they had a hold in them. Quite a few were built as lobster smacks, and those were bigger and had wet wells.

Generally, the width of a Friendship sloop was a third of its length, and a thirty- or thirty-two-footer would draw about six feet. Aside from that, how it was built would be more a matter of preference on the part of the owners, depending on what they were going to use her for. And probably Wilbur Morse would have built you a sloop however you wanted it.

Those early Friendships were built all up and down the Maine coast, but each locality had a little bit different style, much as lobster boats are built today. Just in Muscongus Bay, the Morses did things a little bit different than the McLains, and the differences between localities might have been due to local custom or the conditions the boats were used in. Some builders left out the center-boards and made the hulls deeper, but even into the 1900s they were still building sloops with centerboards for people who fished out of some shoal place, like in the Pool down at Gotts Island.

Sloops built down to Swans Island were generally narrower and deeper than the boats from Friendship. I've seen pictures of some that were built in Brooksville, and they had a little different model than the ones turned out nearby, on Deer Isle.

The early 1900s were the height of the Friendship sloop's activity as a working boat. Right in this area twenty-five of them were registered and sailing out of Southwest Harbor in 1902. Those sloops had to be over five tons to be documented, and there were probably many more smaller ones that were not required to be documented. The local people here used to lobster from Friendship sloops, so they were quite plentiful. It's been said that the light keeper on Baker's Island could count sixty or seventy sails out there on a good day for fishing and lobstering. One man could handle a twenty-five-foot sloop. They generally used the smaller ones for lobstering, although they did fish out of the bigger ones sometimes, and those would have more men, of course.

The old Friendships had an open cockpit and a small cuddy. Those boats were quite low-sided, and the builders put a lot of ballast in them to make them stiff, so they would resist rolling. They sat quite well down in the water, and it was easy enough to haul the traps in over the side. The sloop would heave-to pretty well and lay right there while you hauled your gear. The traps were wooden, and they were bigger than the ones used today.

Motors didn't come in until 1904 or somewhere along in there, and then the builders started putting power in the sloops. They'd generally install the engine down in the cabin and use the original tiller for steering. They'd just run the propeller shaft out through the side, under the flat of her.

Down at Cranberry Island in the early 1900s, the fishermen would use their sloops for lobstering and fishing in the fall, winter, and spring. In the summer they'd haul the boats out, clean them up, paint them, and go sailing summer people. A family would charter a sloop for the season and hire the fisherman to go with it.

Uncle Lew Stanley had two sloops down to Cranberry Island in the early 1900s. One was the *Wanderer,* and one was named the *Volunteer.* He was part owner of another one named the *Gatherer.*

Those old Friendships were originally built real quick and real cheap—for a price and for a purpose. They weren't built to last. The ones that are still around have had a lot of work and restoration done on them.

Probably more Morse sloops have survived because there were so many of them. There were hundreds. But they were the poorest built ones. Morse was producing them for a price, and he built as quick as he could. If you had a thousand dollars and you wanted a thousand-dollar sloop, you could get one. If you had only five hundred dollars, you could buy one for that, but you wouldn't get as much boat.

The McLain sloops were better. Generally, the McLains would build a sloop for themselves and use it one summer and sell it the next fall. Then, over the winter, they'd build another one for the next year. Or they might use a boat two years or three years. But they always built it for themselves, and they were always trying to build the boat better.

Sloops like that were used for fishing and lobstering until just before the beginning of World War II, and most of them were on their last legs when I was growing up. But I do remember them out sailing and being worked. The *Dolphin* was one that belonged to Archie Spurling. Another was the *Sweet Pea,* which belonged to my father's cousin Peter Richardson.

It takes a special person to want a Friendship sloop, somebody that appreciates traditional things. They're a nice boat to sail, and they're an easy boat to sail. They look like they'd be a lot of work, but once you have the sails up and get them going, they're easy.

I've probably made more lobster boats than sloops, but I've built quite a few Friendships and rebuilt quite a few. I suppose I have contributed something to keeping the design alive. In fact, the Friendship Sloop Society gave me an award a few years ago for making a significant contribution towards the preservation and continuation of Friendships.

CHAPTER Fifteen

MY OWN SHOP

In 1973, I rebuilt the *Dictator* for Jarvis Newman. I had wanted a Friendship sloop of my own, and I had known about the *Dictator* for a long while. Every time I went up to Stonington where she was stored, I'd go look at her. She was setting there with a big hole in the bow, just dying.

I had hoped to have her myself, and I'd dreamt about getting her and rebuilding her. But of course I couldn't. The owners wouldn't sell her, and I didn't have any money to buy her anyway. Over on Little Deer Isle there was another old Friendship, that I would like to have had, too. Finally, Jarvis bought the *Dictator* and brought her down here to Southwest Harbor. He hauled

her up into his shop and got me to do the rebuilding. She was thirty-one feet, and she had to be completely redone. Afterwards he took a mold of her to use in building fiberglass Friendships.

It was during that time that I met Ed Kaelber. He was president of the College of the Atlantic in Bar Harbor, and he had bought this old twenty-six-footer sloop called the *Amos Swan*. The boat was a wreck. She didn't even look like a Friendship sloop.

Somebody had sawed the stern off and boarded it up, and the boat had a big, boxy cabin. She had also been retimbered so that there was no shape left to the hull. The *Amos Swan* had a bowsprit on it, the sails were really too

The restored Friendship sloop Dictator *on her mooring in front of Jarvis Newman's house in Manset about 1977.*

small and didn't fit, and the boat was slow. But Kaelber had bought the old thing and wanted me to rebuild her.

When I took the job, I was still working in the old paint shop in back of my grandmother's house. My mother had died in 1969, and then, after my father died in 1971, my sister and her husband bought the property from the estate. So I needed to move out of the old shop, and I looked around for a place to work in. Jarvis said

he would rent me part of his space, so I took the old *Amos Swan* down there.

But there was nothing to rebuild. She was so badly out of shape and she'd been altered so much that you couldn't tell what was there originally. We couldn't even get the model off of her, she was such a mess. She was too far gone.

In the end, we just took off all the hardware and anything else that we could save, and then sawed her up and built Ed another Friendship.

We had her general dimensions, and I designed the new boat following the lines of the *Venture*, which was built about the same time by the same man, Wilbur Morse.

We built the new hull over to Jarvis's and launched her there. In the fall I brought her across the harbor, and we finished her in the storage building behind my house on Clark Point Road.

Kaelber told me later that it appeared to him while I was rebuilding the *Dictator* that I was going to be working for someone else the rest of my life. He thought I shouldn't do that. I might have for a while, but it wouldn't have lasted. Kaelber told me I should keep on with building wooden boats, and his saying that was the push I needed. I already had one building that I stored boats in behind my house, and he proposed that I put up a separate workshop and go out on my own. And that's what I really wanted to do.

So Ed Kaelber put in some money, and we built the new building. I don't think I could have done it without his help. And you know, all through my life, I've had the support of a lot of people. They've encouraged me to do things and keep going.

Of course, I had to borrow money, too. That's when the bankers turned down my application for a loan three times. I think I still had a mortgage on the storage building when I first asked for $17,000, and they wouldn't let me have it. So I waited a couple of weeks and applied again. And they turned me down again. So I applied *again*, and they still didn't want to give me the loan. They thought the boats I had in storage were "just a pain" and felt I should get rid of them and use my existing building to work in.

Jarvis had already told me that he could send over all the hulls that I wanted to finish off. "Well," I answered, "I really don't want to finish off boats. I want to *build* boats."

If I had given up the storage business and used that shed like the bankers said, I'd have been locked into finishing off fiberglass hulls, and that's something I didn't want to do. I'd have been doing work that I didn't have my heart in, and I couldn't do that. I still can't.

So I applied for the loan again, and this time one of the bank's vice presidents came over. I talked with him and told him what I wanted to do, and he looked over what I had here—the boats in the storage building and everything.

I said, "You know, if some winter I didn't happen to get a boat to build, I've got these storage boats that are going to carry me through." He didn't say anything right then, but you could see that the wheels were turning. He went back to the bank, and I got the loan.

All in all, Ed Kaelber was a big influence here, and the fact that he came into my business had a real impact. Something we did as a result was to incorporate. He thought that was a good thing, and he guided me. He was an officer of the corporation for quite a while. When I incorporated, we built the new boat shop, and Marion became my bookkeeper. The kids had pretty well grown up by then.

Kaelber had the *Amos Swan* for several years,

and then one summer he decided he'd sell her. It was about the time of the Friendship sloop race, and I got thinking that maybe the company should buy that boat. I gave him a call on the phone, but he'd already put it in the hands of a broker. Before we could get to the bank and see if we could borrow the money to do it, the broker had sold her to somebody in Camden.

That owner had her down there for a few years, but there came up a storm one time and she chafed her mooring rope and went ashore. One side of her was stove all to pieces. The other side was quite intact, but the engine popped out of her and laid on the beach. Somebody got that. So the new owner lost her right there.

Around 1982, Kaelber wanted to sell his shares in the business to me. I didn't have the money right then and there, but my son Richard did. I told Richard he might buy those shares and get a stake in the company. He wanted to and that's what he did, shortly after he got out of boatbuilding school in Eastport.

CHAPTER Sixteen

FRIENDSHIPS OLD AND NEW

With the old Friendship sloops that I've rebuilt, I've changed some of the construction and made it stronger. As far as the lines go, though, I have stuck to the original design as well as I could. I haven't tried to change the model a great deal.

Some of the early sloops would drag their stern down if you sailed them hard. They'd heel over, and the bow would rise. The stern wasn't buoyant enough, so it would go down and water would come in over the coaming. Some of those Friendships were sunk that way. Most of the later sloops didn't have that problem. The builders filled them out and made them wider and more buoyant back aft. I've pretty much followed the later models of the sloops. It's mostly in the manner of construction that I've made changes.

As I've said, those old boats weren't meant to last forever. They were built for a few years' use, and when they were worn out you'd get another one. Back then, there was plenty of wood and plenty of labor. Boats were inexpensive. Today it's different. The lumber's scarcer, the fastenings cost more, and you expect the boat to last longer. We try to build them so they will.

In 1975, James Russell Wiggins brought the *Amity* down for me to rebuild. I think Jarvis Newman might have had something to do with that. I had gone over to Brooklin with him one time to talk with Mr. Wiggins, but it was some-

Robert Wolfe, who had Morning Star *restored.*

time later that Mr. Wiggins came to me about the *Amity.* By then, our daughter Nadine's husband, Tim Goodwin, had started working for me. We saved the deck, but then we rebuilt the hull almost from the sheer down. A lot of that deck was in the way when we were working on the rest of her.

Then, in 1976, a man named Robert Wolfe came in about a sloop called the *Morning Star.* She was down in Camden, and I had to have her trucked over here. I'm not completely sure about her history, but someone once told me there was

a *Morning Star* over to Winter Harbor. She was forty-some feet and built by Wilbur Morse. But this sloop was built by Wilbur's brother, Albion, or at least that's what her trailboards said when we took her apart.

The *Morning Star* wasn't big enough to be documented, so there were no numbers on her in order to trace the ownership back. We do know that she was built in Cushing and that she had been rebuilt a number of times. She had really been butchered, but you could tell pretty much how she was originally built. About all we saved was the shape, the model. We did take a piece of the old keel and fasten it on the bulkhead. That's what was original. There were some things that I didn't do as she was originally done, and some things I did better than they were originally done. The fastenings we used were different, for instance. We used bronze instead of galvanized iron.

About that time, along came Dick Dudman, and he wanted a brand-new Friendship. The *Freedom* was built on my own lines. We already had the *Morning Star* in the shop, tearing her apart. We planked her up, and then we set up the *Freedom* and planked her up. We finished the two sloops together.

I had taken Dick and Helen Dudman out in *Hieronymus* back in the mid-'60s, I guess. He was then a journalist with the *St. Louis Post-Dispatch,* and he had a summer house on Little Cranberry Island. His children were in college, and he didn't have a great deal of money, so he didn't have a boat built at that time. But he still

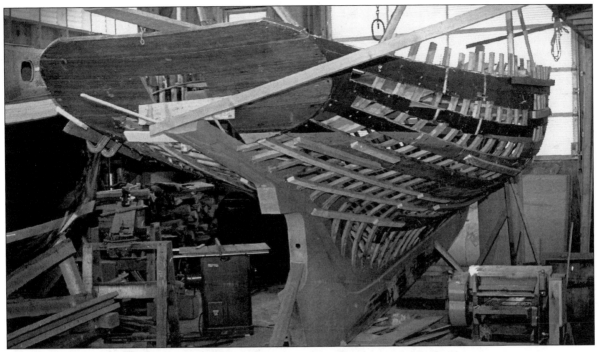

Morning Star had alternate planks removed during rebuilding (above).

Putting the "fashion piece" in place as the planking nears completion.

91

Moving Morning Star *(in her cradle) onto our marine railway for launching.*

Morning Star *is launched.*

liked Friendships and thought he wanted one.

Then Dick was over in Viet Nam and Cambodia on assignment, and he got captured with some other newspeople. He was marched around as a prisoner for a month or more, never knowing what might happen. He made up his mind that if he ever got out of that mess, he was going to have a Friendship sloop. So when he got home, he came to me and we talked about a twenty-eight-footer, which we built. That was the *Freedom*, and he's still got her.

The next year, in 1977, we built a twenty-six-foot sloop for Peter P. Blanchard III on the same lines as the *Amos Swan*. He originally came to

Richard and me on board the newly launched Morning Star.

me through Will Neilson, Albie's son. We made an appointment to go out in Kaelber's boat. The day that we were to take her out, I had her across the head of the town dock, and there was not much wind. They came down, Peter and his father, and piled aboard.

The father was awfully uncomfortable on a boat as a result of some childhood experiences, but I just cast off and sailed right away from the dock. We tacked out and went around the harbor and came back in. We never had to start the motor at all, and everything was fine. The Blanchards were amazed that we could do that. That's when they said they wanted a boat *exactly* like the *Amos Swan.*

I said, "There's a few things I'd like to change."

"Oh, no!" they said. "Don't change a thing! We want one *exactly* the same."

So I built the *Peregrine* just as near as I could. But even if you try to build one boat exactly like another, it's bound to look a little different and handle a little differently. Most people can't tell, but I can.

A boat is the nearest thing you can build to something that's living. A house just sits on the ground and stays put. But a boat moves from place to place, and it has a life and a spirit of its own. When you're handling a boat, it feels like a living thing.

The "sister ships" Morning Star *and* Freedom *sailing off Mount Desert Island on a beautiful October day.*

Dick Dudman and me during the
Friendship Sloop Regatta.

All this time, I really wanted a Friendship of my own. Years before, I had talked to Bill Pendleton, who was president of the Friendship Sloop Society and owner of the *Black Jack*. I had told him that I'd like to have a Friendship but that I didn't know how I would ever do it. The kids were little and I didn't have any money. And Bill says, "Well, go without something and get your Friendship! Build that boat!"

So I always had it in the back of my mind that if I ever got the opportunity I would. In 1979, I got a thirty-six-foot passenger boat to build, and on the spur of the moment I also ordered enough lumber to build a Friendship on speculation. The bank was

Launch day for Endeavor *in 1979, with* Freedom *alongside.*

very unhappy with me because I owed them some money, and instead of paying them back, I bought that lumber. But I had never missed a payment, and they really couldn't say anything. In the end they renewed my notes, so it worked out all right.

That Friendship was the *Endeavor,* and she's twenty-five feet. She was built with an open cockpit and originally had inside ballast. Now she's got all lead inside, but I used all beach rocks at that time. I worked as cheap as I could to keep the cost down, so I just picked up rocks to put in her. Back when they built the old Friendships, the fishermen liked a boat that had inside ballast, because even though it might roll deeper, it rolled slower. A sloop

Richard and I load stone ballast.

95

The battery-sailer Summer Joy.

that had outside ballast would snap back upright quick, like a pendulum.

I had intended to keep the *Endeavor* for myself, at least for a while, and I'd probably still have her if I hadn't gotten in a bind and sold her. Anyway, it turned out all right in the end. When I had to sell her, she went to a man down to Harrington.

He had her for two summers, then he put her up for sale. His wife didn't like him being out by himself so much, and she didn't want to go in

that boat. It didn't have room enough for her, and she wanted to get something that she could go in, too. So we put the word out about the *Endeavor*, and within a week or so I had it sold. Betsey Holtzmann of Southwest Harbor owns her now and keeps her moored right off our dock.

I've also built three nineteen-foot sailboats that are related in design to the Friendship sloops. This little sloop sails like a bigger boat and feels like a heavier boat. I built a little weather helm in her on purpose, to make her safer for young people to sail. If they get hit with a gust, she'll come right up into the wind.

The hull form is quite similar to a Friendship, but the nineteen-footer has a round bow, and the rig is a little bit different. It's just a single jib because this is a small boat. The boom is shorter, and the mast is taller and set farther aft. But the design is similar enough that the Friendship Sloop Society accepts them as Friendship sloops.

The first nineteen-footer I built was for Peter Forbes's son Alex, in 1985. That was the *Bucephalus*. She's built like the old catboats, with up-and-down staves running inside the coaming to the bottom of the boat. She had all inside ballast, and we put a club topsail on her

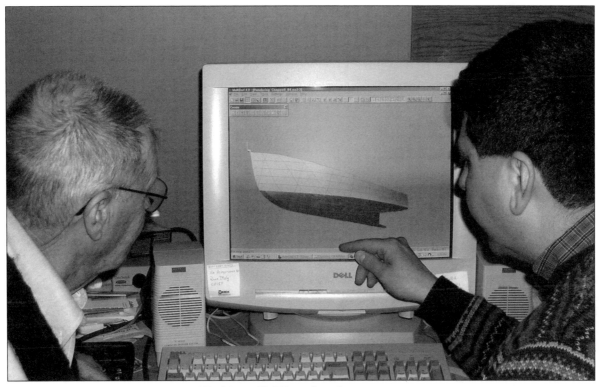

Working with Edward on the computer.

after we built her, so Alex could get a little more speed out of the boat.

The second nineteen-footer was for the Strouds, and that was the *Little Folly*, in 1986. The third was the *Summer Joy* for the Kleinschmidts, which we finished in 1989. That boat was a little unusual because it had an electric motor with six, twelve-volt automotive batteries inside. That was quite a lot of weight.

I've adapted the basic design a couple of times to make a larger or smaller boat. The *Dovekie*, which we built for Frank Newlin in 1988, was the nineteen-footer expanded to twenty-eight feet. In 1995, I stretched those lines to twenty-one feet for Mrs. Franchetti. There's also a little sixteen-footer that we built for Mike Rindler. She's a scaled-*down* version of the

nineteen-footer. That boat is named the *Timothy M.,* and we launched her in 1997.

The first full-size Friendship sloop we'd produced since the *Endeavor*, in 1979, was the *Acadia*, which we finished in 1998. She was built for Adrian Edmondson and her homeport is Dartmouth, England. He wanted the boat just like the *Endeavor*, only twenty-eight feet instead of twenty-five-and-a-half. I just scaled up the dimensions of the *Endeavor*, but I had to make a new hull shape, and I drafted her lines all new.

For the *Acadia*, I did it all on paper, but we've got that design in the computer now. We have a PC with design software on it, and my son Edward helps me with that. Once you've got a set of lines in the computer, you can loft the boat out full size. That's a big advantage.

They already have some of my designs in the plans repository down at Mystic Seaport. Eventually, I'd like to take all my lines that are just on paper and getting worn out, and put them into the computer. Then when people come in, I can show them these plans and turn the lines inside out and upside down.

I guess someday I may learn how to use the computer myself, but I can fair-out a set of lines on paper easily and twice as quick. I really like sitting at the drawing board and working out the lines on paper.

Acadia *under sail on October 6, 1998.*

CHAPTER *Seventeen*

MY OTHER BOATS

There's never been any pattern to which type of boat I was going to build next. It was mostly what came along. Besides the lobster boats and Friendship sloops, there have been a few others that were interesting to work on.

In 1978, I got the job to rebuild an old R-class racing sloop for a member of the Rockefeller family. That was the *Jack Tar*. She was originally built in City Island, New York, in 1916 I believe, and the Rockefellers got her in 1920. That sloop stayed in the family for years, but they finally sold her after they had a fiberglass boat built. The man who bought the *Jack Tar* took her to Portland and had her down there for a while. He had quite a lot of work done on her

from time to time. Then he got transferred to the West Coast, so he put her up for sale and the Rockefellers bought the boat back.

They sailed her around that summer and then brought the sloop to me. By that time she really needed to be rebuilt, and that was quite a little job. Even the lead keel had to be melted down and recast. But she still sailed nice. You could take that boat when it was calm and just give her a push and she'd go forever.

Every R-class sloop was a little different. Some had the mast stepped way aft. Some had the mast stepped way forward. And they were all sizes. That was fine, as long as they conformed to the rule that was written to rate these sail-

Peter Godfrey sailing the Rose.

boats. Naturally, whenever somebody makes a rule like that, all the naval architects try to build a boat that will beat it.

We didn't have the original plans to go by but, of course, we had the old boat. When we pulled her apart, we took every other timber out and every other plank off. We put new timbers in, and then we replanked her. By doing it that way we could keep the shape about the way it was originally. The *Jack Tar* turned out pretty good.

In 1982, I built a twenty-eight-foot boat called the *Rose* for Peter Godfrey. She was based on L. Francis Herreshoff's design for the *Rozinante*, which is called a canoe yawl but is actually a ketch. She had a teak deck, and she was really quite a fancy boat.

Peter had Herreshoff's plans, and that boat had always interested me, from way back when I first saw her in *Rudder* magazine and read about her as a kid. But there were some parts that I didn't like, and when I built the *Rose*, I had the opportunity to change those and do it my own way.

Herreshoff's original *Rozinante* was designed to be built with a skeg that came straight down from the deadwood. I changed that and made the boat with a built-down keel. That gave her a wineglass shape and made her much stronger.

I didn't like some of Herreshoff's way of fastening things together, either, like fastening the keel on with lag screws. So I used bolts. I made the boat a little heavier, too, but the top of her looked the same.

In 1983, I built a little schooner for Henry Sage Goodwin. He was an older fella that had a little Friendship sloop he had stored down to Southwest Boat for quite a while. He came in

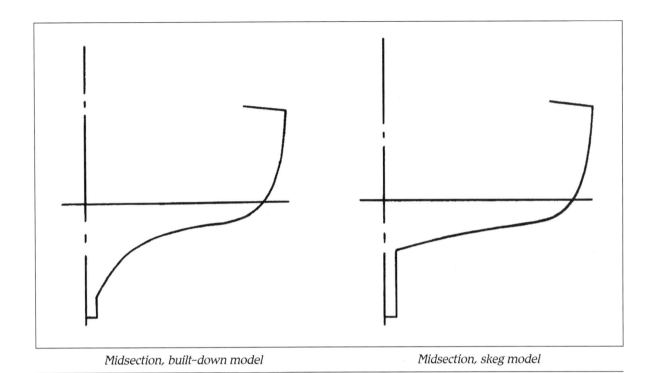

| Midsection, built-down model | Midsection, skeg model |

here one day and said that he thought his boat would be more happy alongside other Friendship sloops. So he brought her up here, and we stored her for the winter.

We kept Goodwin's boat for several winters, actually, and did some work on her. Then he sold her, and I figured he was all done sailing. He was quite lame and walked with a cane and had a bad hip. But he came in one day, and he said, "I've decided I'm going to have a schooner built." He told me what he wanted and we worked out the plans and I built her. She was a twenty-eight-foot centerboarder, shoal draft.

It seems to me Goodwin's wife died midway in the building of that boat. Then his good hip went bad, and he had that replaced. But we got the boat off, and he sailed her here in Southwest Harbor for about five years. Then he decided he wanted her in Mystic, Connecticut. I had her

trucked down, and he got somebody to take care of her there.

Goodwin sailed her down there a little bit, and then he decided he'd give her to Mystic Seaport. They had her for a while, and then they sold her to a fella in Westerly, Rhode Island, a man whose wife worked at Mystic Seaport. He kept the schooner in a tidal pond down in Westerly, and then in the wintertime he stored her at the Seaport. He had that boat for a number of years until he died. Then his widow put her up for sale, and Dennis Kavanagh here in town heard about it. He bought her and brought her back. So she's right here now.

That same year, we finished up a twelve-foot rowboat that I'd been building for a long time for Hank Neilson. He had an old Arthur Spurling boat, and I took the lines off of that and built him a new one.

The Belle

Arthur Spurling lived to be more than a hundred. He had sold his house when he was eighty-odd years old. The fella that bought the place told him he could stay there the rest of his life, and Arthur lived another twenty years. He almost outlived the man that bought it. Arthur was related to me through the Stanleys and the Bunkers. I had met him when I was growing up. He was still building boats up into the 1940s, but I never got to his shop. I don't know exactly when he stopped.

In 1994, we built a flat-bottomed riverboat called *Belle* for Holyoke Whitney. He wanted her long and narrow, so she's twenty-five feet long and five feet wide. I designed her special. Whitney had already cruised the lower

The Resolute

Mississippi, and he wanted to do the upper Mississippi. That riverboat's about the only thing that was completely different than anything I'd ever designed before.

In 1996, we completed a sailboat called the *Resolute* that I designed for Hugh Harwood. He had been talking with me for ten years about a cutter, and I first made him a half model that hung in his office. He finally came around to have the boat built. She wasn't built exactly from the half-model, but she's similar.

The *Resolute* is a typical English-style cutter, long and narrow with a deep keel and a long bowsprit. With a cutter, the mast is usually stepped about a third of the way from the bow to the stern. The stem is plumb, and there's a long overhang on the stern with a little, fine, narrow transom. It usually has a small staysail jib forward of the mast and a topsail on the main, but we rigged Hugh's boat with a club topsail.

The next year, we built a twenty-eight-foot schooner for Roger Duncan, the maritime historian, and his wife, Mary. That boat was a new

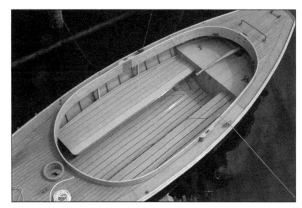

Resolute's *cockpit*

design, although in profile she's similar to the *Dovekie*, which was a Friendship type, open sail boat that we had finished in 1988. Roger's boat has the same transom and the same underwater profile as the *Dovekie*, but without quite as much sheer.

During the time we were building that boat, Roger was in a swimming pool down in Boothbay, and he knew there was something wrong. He got out of the water and said someone had better take him to the doctor. They rushed him to the hospital in Boothbay, and the people there recognized that he had an aneurism. They

Roger and Mary Duncan at Boothbay with their schooner.

The Dorothy Elizabeth

took him right to Portland, and the doctors there decided they had to operate right quick.

I didn't find out about it for a few days. I called up for some guidance on the boat, and Mary told me what had happened. Then I didn't know what the Duncans would do—whether they'd keep on with the boat or not—but we stayed working on it.

Roger had a phone in his hospital room in Portland, so I called him up when I could. He sounded pretty weak, but every time I'd talk about the boat, his voice would sound stronger and he'd perk right up. Mary said that thinking about the schooner kept him going.

We built the hull for him and finished the deck and put the engine in. Then we ran her down to Boothbay, and he took her from there. We had to furnish the masts for him, and he was a year or so getting her rigged, but he got it done. He spliced all the wire himself. When he got the masts in her, he put her off.

The name of the boat is the *Dorothy Elizabeth.* She was named for his mother and his wife's mother. Marion and I went down to the launching. Later in the year, in the fall, we went down and had a sail on her. She handles pretty good.

CHAPTER *Eighteen*

MY CUSTOMERS

You never know where your next customer is going to come from, and sometimes it's a matter of being in the right place at the right time.

One time I just happened to be here in Southwest on Labor Day because I was waiting to go to the hospital to have two hernias fixed. Marion had gone off somewhere with her sister. I was in the office, and in came this couple from Massachusetts. They'd been over to Belfast looking at a boat, and the builder had taken them out in it.

It was quite fast, and the builder had said, "This boat'll do fifty knots if you put enough power in it." I guess they'd had quite a ride, and that wasn't what they wanted to hear. It seems that previously they'd had a big Boston Whaler down in Buzzards Bay, and the wife had bounced off the seat and come back down and badly bruised her backside. It was awful painful, and they didn't want anything like that again.

So I dug out some plans and showed them what I could build and what it would cost and what the power would be. I showed them one of my boats in the water, too. They wanted to know how fast it would go, and I said, "Well, probably fifteen knots, but there'll be a lot of times when you won't want to go that fast. Eight knots is a good speed some days." Apparently that's what they wanted to hear, because before they left they decided to have a boat built.

The Annie T

That winter, after I had the hernias fixed, I built a twenty-nine-foot powerboat for them. The timber for the keel was outside between the buildings—this was in December—and I wasn't supposed to do anything for quite a while. My shoulder had frozen up, too. I couldn't lift my arm up very high, and I had to go to physical therapy.

But I had that keel setting out there, and I wanted to square it up. The shop was full at that moment, so I decided I'd do it outside. I got dressed up warm and went out and worked on that keel right there. When I told the doctor what I was up to, he said, "Well, that's the best thing you can do."

As soon as we could, we brought the keel into the shop and built the boat. The couple took her down to Massachusetts, and they were quite happy with her. The next year they brought her back here on a cruise. As far as I know, they've still got the boat. I don't know just how they'd heard about me, but if I hadn't been here that Labor Day, I'd have missed them.

People that come in for a wooden boat know boats and understand boats. They know pretty much what they want, and they know that they might have to wait several months or even a year for the boat to be built. You enter into a kind of a partnership with them as to how you're going to lay out the space below decks and what you're going to include and so on.

Years ago, when a lobsterman would come in, he was usually a person that already had a boat and had been planning on having a new one built in a certain year. He'd know about what he wanted for size and everything, and I'd build it. A few fellas that had never been fishing before came in and wanted boats, but they also knew pretty much what they were looking for.

I've generally had good luck with customers over the years, and I've been able to work pretty well with most lobster fishermen. But there were a couple of exceptions. Some of these fellas are pretty rugged individuals, and they have their own ideas.

One of them thought he could slip off with a fishing boat before he finished paying for it. I was afraid he was going to take it out of state, so I had to put a lien on the boat and have a U.S. Marshall put a tag on her, lock her up. I might have been paid eventually, but the way it ended up, I got about four thousand out of the twelve that he owed on it. But the boat turned out good. She's still going.

Another time I built a big forty-four-foot lobster boat for a fella here in town that I'd known practically all my life, since he was a little kid. I'd done some work for him now and then on his old boat and had helped him out. He'd helped me out here in the shop, too. He wanted a bigger boat, and we had talked about it for quite a while.

One year I didn't have a boat to build, and I thought it would be a good chance to start that big one. He allowed that it would, and we drew up a contract. He was supposed to do so much labor on the boat, and I would do so much labor.

When we came to the end of it, he owed $30,000 and wouldn't pay it. At the time, I thought the best thing to do was launch the boat and then either try to get it settled or get a lawyer and bring suit. In the end we did sue, but then I offered to make a settlement for $20,000. I told my lawyer, "If he won't take twenty, go down to fifteen and we'll settle it, get it over with, and for-

get it." But that lobsterman wouldn't talk about a settlement of any kind.

This all started in 1981 and didn't get settled till 1986. It was wearing. I lived with it day and night. I'd think about it when I went to bed at night and think about it when I'd get up in the morning. It had quite a lasting impact on me.

That's one thing about building boats. Even though you're having difficulties with the owner or running short of money or going over budget, you seem obsessed about finishing the boat regardless. It means more to you to get it done than the money means. When you're building a boat, it becomes part of you. That's sometimes a drawback, because you lose your perspective on how much money you're going to get. The next thing you know, you're putting more time into it than you're getting paid for. It's a trap that all boatbuilders fall into.

For me, the ideal customer is the person who will come in and say, "Build me a boat" and who doesn't care what it costs. They tell you what they want, and you can go from there. Usually things will turn out right when you do it that way.

WHEN TIMES WERE THE LOWEST

I never really thought about giving up boat-building, but there was one year where nothing came along and it was pretty tough going. In 1982 I had built the *Rose*, a Herreshoff canoe yawl for Peter Godfrey, and the next year I had built the *Equinox*, a little schooner for Henry Sage Goodwin. That work kept us going for a while, but then things were kind of slack.

That was also the year that I had a kidney stone. On Christmas morning I woke up about three o'clock, and by four I decided it was time to get some help, so I called the hospital. They said, "Come over, but don't try to drive. Get somebody to bring you."

I called my son-in-law, Tim. It was slippery that morning, and he was quite a while coming. I thought, "It's just too icy to make Tim drive over there. I'll call the ambulance." When they arrived, they sat outside and talked on their walkie-talkies for hours it seemed, although it was probably as much as ten minutes. I set out to say, "Let's get this thing rolling!"

They finally got me over to the hospital. The doctors kept me there for a couple of days drinking water, and they were giving me shots. That didn't do anything. So they sent me home with a bottle of pills, and I lay on the couch for about a week. Finally, I passed the stone, and that's the same winter we built the *Folly* on speculation. I borrowed some money, not from a bank but from a private individual, and built this little twenty-one-footer. She was my version of a Herreshoff Fish Class sailboat.

Someone had talked with me previously about building one, and I had looked it up and had gotten interested in the plans. As it turned out, that fella didn't have the boat built, but I liked it anyway, and I thought I would design something similar. So I did.

I didn't copy the Herreshoff plans exactly. The boat looks similar, but it's a little heavier construction. And I didn't have a set of lines to go by, so I just made them up out of my head. The sheer and the profile are about the same, but the rig is a little different, and the hull is different underwater. The original one had a flat keel, parallel with the waterline. I did away with that and put drag in the keel, making it sloping. That helps the boat turn better.

This job kept my crew busy, and I launched her hoping somebody'd come along and buy her. I had that boat for sale all summer, and I had told Mr. Stroud about it. He and his brother wanted to sail in her, so I went out with them one day. We took the twenty-one-footer off the mooring and were tacking out of the harbor when we came right close by a big Hinckley sailboat. We sailed along the side of her from the stern to the bow, and this fella was on board looking at us. He followed us right along his deck, clear to the bow.

He says, "What a pretty boat! What a pretty boat!"

We got out of earshot and Mr. Stroud's brother asks me, "How much did you have to pay him to say that?"

Mr. Stroud didn't say anything about buying the boat right then, but in the fall Mrs. Stroud called up and wanted to know if I would take them out to Placentia Island in it. I said "Sure," so they came over and we sailed out there to see someone they knew. When we got back here and were coming up the dock, Mr. Stroud says to Mrs. Stroud, "What are we going to do? Are we going to buy that boat or what?" They talked about it and decided, yes, they were going to buy that boat.

They wrote me a check for a down payment and sent me the remainder when they got back to Pennsylvania. Then, two or three months later, I got *another* check. They'd forgotten that they'd given me the final payment. Well, I got right on the telephone, cranked her up, and told Mrs. Stroud what had happened.

"Oh," she says, "just throw it away. Tear it up."

And I said, "I'll send the check back to you."

"No, no, no. Don't do that. Just tear it up. Throw it away."

It was awful hard to tear up that check, but I did.

The Strouds had also talked about having another boat built to use over to their camp at Pretty Marsh, but that didn't happen right away. In the meantime, I built the little nineteen-foot sailboat called the *Bucephalus*. After I got that off, I was in hard straights for a while there. I owed the bank a lot of money because I was in that lawsuit over the forty-four-foot lobsterboat, and it was still pending for $30,000. That was when the bank called me up one day and wanted to talk with me.

I went over there, and they said, "We know you're having a hard time, and we want to help you out." I had several long-term and short-term notes, so they were going to make a proposal. They wanted to consolidate all those notes into one big long-term note—at 19.75 percent. Well, I knew that would ruin me. I didn't even have to think about it to realize that with a note that big at an interest rate that high, I'd be bankrupt within a few months. But I said, "Let me think it over."

They said, "Sure. Take a couple of weeks."

So, I went out through the bank door, and I thought, "What can I do?"

I had the *Endeavor*, my own Friendship sloop, so I sold her and got enough money to make substantial payments on some of my short-term notes. That brought my debt down quite a bit, and I said to the bank, "Let's keep it just the way it is for a while longer." And they said okay. They went along a little while, but then they called me in again and wanted to do the same thing—only this time the rate was 14.75 percent. So I called up Mr. Stroud, and I said, "Have you thought any more about that boat you wanted for Pretty Marsh?"

Well, no, he and Mrs. Stroud hadn't thought any more about it. He didn't know whether they would go ahead or not.

So I told him, "Well, if you wanted one, this would be a good time to do it."

Mr. Stroud wanted to know why, and I said, "I don't have anything to build, and I've got a little problem with the bank." I told him what they wanted to do.

"Oh, well," he says, "let's have that boat! And I tell you what we'll do. We'll send you some money to start it with. We'll also send you more towards the future upkeep of the boat."

I took him up on that. Then I borrowed some money on a life-insurance policy to make a loan payment big enough to hold off the bank, and I carried it over there. They were some surprised. It was a sizeable sum, and they hadn't expected it. They thought they had me on the barrel. Sometime later, I found out there were people in town that wanted my property. In any event, the bank went along with it. They couldn't do any different, because my record of payment was pretty good.

Soon after that I won the lawsuit. It took a year to collect, but finally I paid off everything, except for one long-term note that I'd had for some time. I kept that right to the bitter end, at 9 percent. The bank agreed to that rate when they took on the loan. They thought they were getting a good deal in the beginning, but after 19.75 percent interest came in, they didn't think it was so good any more.

Anyway, I got clear of that mess and built the Strouds that other nineteen-foot sailboat called the *Little Folly*.

While I was still in the lawsuit, Mrs. Stroud had called me up one Friday. It was the Fourth

The Little Folly

took her to New York, and she died of cancer two days later. I always thought it was really something that she'd had one foot in the grave and she was worried about me. But that's the way she was. Mrs. Stroud was an awfully nice person.

That whole period was about my lowest point. As I've said, it was hard scratchin' because of all the money that was tied up in that forty-four-footer and in the lawsuit—and because I had no other boats to build.

It might have been easier just to give up boat-building, but at that point in my life I was too old to jump into something else. And then I had my son-in-law Tim working for me and my daughter Nadine was doing the bookkeeping and my son Richard was here. There were other fellas working for me, too, and I didn't want to just let them go. Luckily, I had the storage boats, and that helped keep things going.

During the time we were building the big lobster boat, Tim and I found a place where some hackmatack trees were dying. Each weekend we were able to cut enough for firewood to last in the shop for a week or so. I also put some down cellar to use in the stove to help heat the house. That cut the oil bill down quite a bit. Lugging out those big hackmatack pieces was where I got my two hernias. But we got through.

of July weekend, and I was going to court the following Monday up in Ellsworth. She was worried about me, and said she'd gotten her nephew, who was a lawyer, to confer with my lawyer and help out a little bit.

Monday morning I was waiting to go to court when Steve Spurling came in the shop saying Mrs. Stroud had died. She'd been sick, and the night she'd talked with me she got worse. They

CHAPTER *Twenty*

ABOUT DESIGNING BOATS

I've been doing boat-design work since I was about thirteen years old, and I'm pretty much self-taught. The only formal training I had was when I studied mechanical drawing in the seventh and eighth grades.

By that time, I had set up a sort of drafting table at home and was drawing boat lines and construction plans for different boats that I had in my head. Back then, Southwest Boat was building commercial fishing boats, and I spent lots of time over there looking at them to see how they were constructed.

I'd always puzzled about how lines drawings could represent the actual shape of a boat. For a long time, it was something I couldn't under-

stand. But one day I was on my bicycle down on the town dock, and all of a sudden it came to me. It was just as clear as could be how those lines blended into the shape of a boat. I had it all figured out, just like that!

Drawing lines came easily to me, and all through high school I designed a lot of boats. I guess it was just after the war that Arthur Moore and I decided to build a big model of a dragger. He and I were schoolmates. I was about sixteen when I drew the lines for it and he started building it. The model was about four or five feet long.

That summer, Arthur worked at Southwest Boat, painting. They were building a real dragger there, so he got to see how it was done, with the

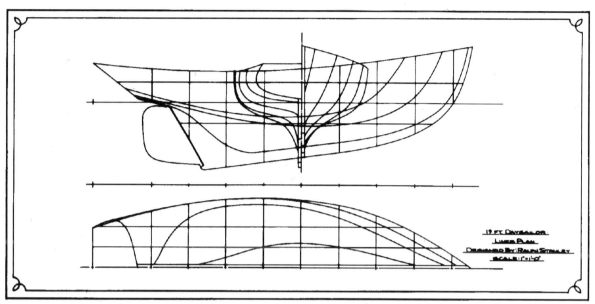

Lines plan for the nineteen-footer.

blocks on the deck and the wires running to the winches. It was long after school was over that he finally got our model finished, but he did and he's still got it. I built a model schooner myself once, but that model dragger was probably the only boat to get built from anything I'd designed until I built a real lobster boat for myself when I was twenty-one.

Back then, when I was getting started, Alden and Herreshoff were still alive. I wish I'd gone to talk with them, but they were far away when I was twenty-one years old. They were in Boston or Marblehead, and I didn't think I'd ever get there. I'd like to have seen how they worked—their drafting tables, and their tools. In those days I might even have liked working for them. But it was the end of the era of wooden-boat design, and there wasn't much going on after that.

It's hard to say where design ideas come

from. Usually, if somebody wants me to build them a boat, I get the length and the width and I find out how they're going to use it. Then I just think about what it should look like, and I put it on paper.

When I design a boat, I usually start with the profile. Then I draw the sheer line and what I think the waterline ought to look like. Then I put some sections in between, from the bow to the midsection to the stern. Next, I draw some buttock lines and see if they fair out, then I keep adjusting them until they do, until I get it the way I want it. There's a lot of visualization to it. You've got to see the completed boat in your head, the shape of it and everything, and I seem to be able to do that easily. I've always had an eye for the shape.

When I go about designing a boat, I sometimes make half models out of wood. If I'm in a

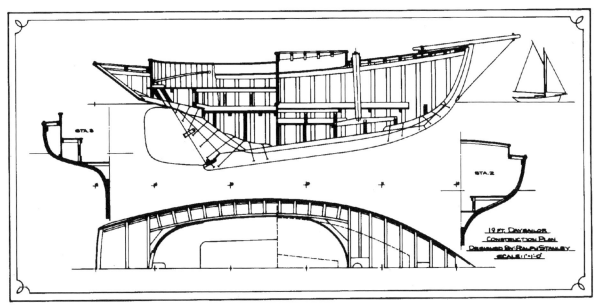

Construction plan for the nineteen-footer.

hurry, I just draw out a set of lines on paper. But a model shows the shape of the boat and how it's going to look when it's finished. Then you can take measurements off of the model and scale them up to do your lofting or to make the molds that you set up at stations along the keel when you're building.

That's the same thing the old builders did. Sometimes they actually sawed the model into sections and then traced those profiles out on paper to get their stations. But I generally have made a template to fit the side of the model, and then I use that template to transfer the profiles to paper. Once I get the stations transferred, I draw out all the rest. You generally have three or four buttock lines. Those are as if you sliced the boat lengthwise a certain distance from the centerline. The waterlines are as if the model was sliced longitudinally, on the waterline and at certain dis-

tances above or below the waterline.

Sometimes I play with designs on the drawing board, but generally I do my best when somebody comes and actually wants a boat. Then I try to get a good sheer line and try to design something that'll hold the weight where they want to put it, something that'll be a good sea boat. Let's say a fella wants a twenty-six-footer like the *Annie T*, but he needs to put more power in her. I'll design a boat that will take a little bit more weight. I've already got a plan that I can hunt up and show him. We'll look at it and we'll talk about it and modify it to fit what he needs.

Now, if this fella doesn't want anything fancy, maybe we can do it right up quick—in four or five months or so. We might start building in, say, November and finish in April. That works good if we can do it. I have built two that way in one winter.

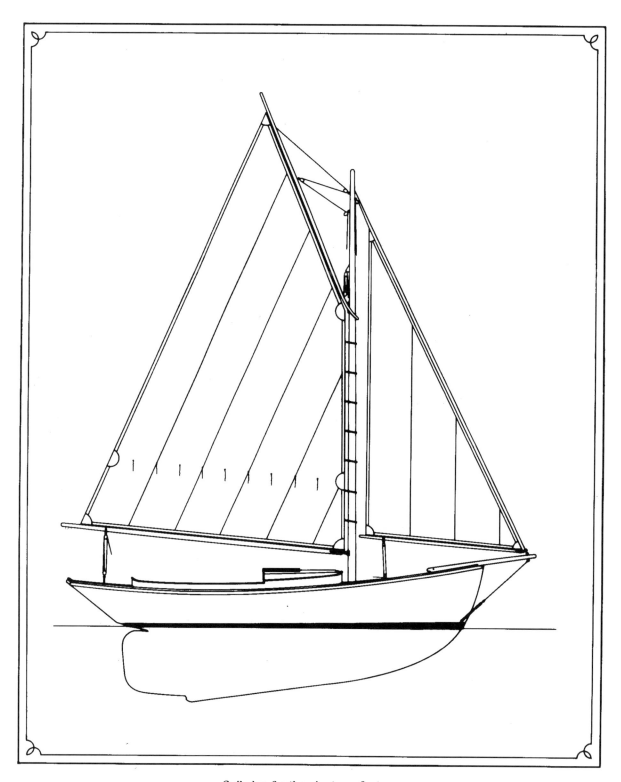

Sail plan for the nineteen-footer.

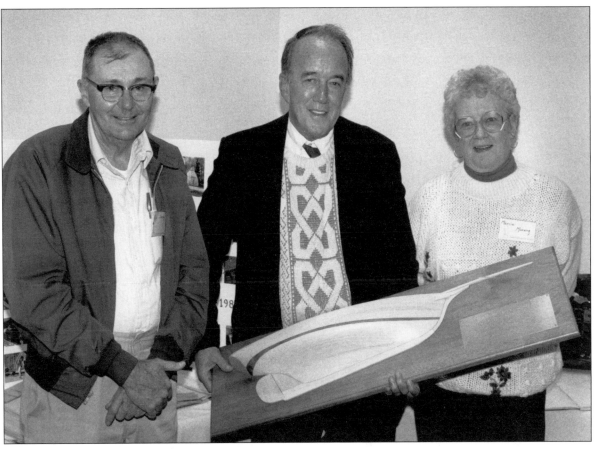

Bruce and Marcia Morang were presented with a half-model I made as an award at the Friendship Sloop Society annual meeting in 1992.

A good wooden boat has got to be built solid, have good materials in it. It's got to have a good model, and it's got to be arranged so you can work out of it. How it's rigged depends on what the customer needs to use it for, too. Sometimes you have to change the model a little bit for what the buyer wants, and sometimes you see where you'd want to change it yourself.

Different people have different ideas about the best height from the platform—some call it the deck—to the bottom edge of the coaming, for example. Usually the fishermen want it so that their knee comes *under* the coaming. If your knee

hits right *on* the coaming, it's awful irritating, and it'll eat your kneecap out in time.

Where to put the engine is a big thing, too. So is locating the fuel tanks and things like that. Some fellas want their tanks under the stern deck, and some want them under the platform. Some want a long stern deck, and some want a short one. It's all according to what their preference is.

One fella wanted his side deck just wide enough so that he could put his dinner pail on it endways. That way, when he rowed up alongside to get aboard, his dinner pail would stay there even if the water was choppy. If it only fit sideways, it would have rolled overboard, because the Thermos bottle in the top of it was heavy. But endways you could cram it in between the coaming and the rail, and it would stay there. That fella had owned one boat where the deck wasn't wide enough for his dinner pails by half an inch, and he lost a lot of them overboard that way.

On fishing boats, the height of the steering wheel is another thing. It's got to be low enough so that water doesn't run along your arms. If you get the wheel too high, your arms are up and water's running down your elbows all the time because your hands are wet.

Being around boats all your life and being on them is quite a big part in designing them. I've been able to look at a planked-up boat with no mark on it and put my finger on the bow where the actual waterline's going to fall. I don't know how I can do this, but I've been able to come out pretty close. Raymond Bunker could, too. He could tell you where a boat was going to set in the water by just looking at the hull.

You have to have experience to do this, and I suppose that even when I was a kid building toy boats and floating them in ponds and finding out how they set, I was getting experience. And when you sail one of your own boats and watch how it handles, that influences the next one you're going to design, too.

I've always had strong feelings about my own models, especially the lobster boats. When I design a boat, it's unique. It's mine. There's no other like it. It has to do with the shape, the sheer, the way I put things together, and the little things I do that nobody else does, that nobody else can do.

CHAPTER *Twenty-one*

FIBERGLASS OR WOOD?

As I've said, there's not much demand for wooden workboats today. I hadn't built one since 1983, and then in 1999 we got an order to build a new forty-four-footer for commercial fishing, but that's the exception.

That's partly because it's easier for people to buy and maintain fiberglass, but it's also because the price of a wooden boat scares most people to death. For some reason, they think they can get a wooden boat cheap because they think wood is somehow inferior. But it doesn't work that way.

To build a wooden hull to the point of a finished fiberglass hull, you've got a lot more work into it. It's not just the time and materials involved, it's also the skill. A wooden lobster boat, if she's real fancy, is about comparable in price with a glass boat all finished. You could have $250,000 or more in it with the electronics and all the other gear you want to put in.

So the market for wooden boats today is mostly limited to pleasure boats and individuals who like wood and trust wood. It's people who want something that's the best, a museum piece. They want a real fine finish, and the cost doesn't scare them.

Now, the average person might not think it matters whether a boat is made of fiberglass or wood. But there are differences. Even though the glass boat and the wooden boat will weigh the same and even sit on the waterline in the same

Planing the garboard plank for the Freedom.

easier to stand on. It doesn't transmit the vibration of the engine as much.

Nevertheless, when fiberglass came in, I gave some serious thought to building a mold and turning out fiberglass boats, and we did finish a fiberglass hull here in my shop once. It was one of the Newman 32s that I had modeled for Jarvis. But I got thinking about it, and with every boat that I had ever built, I could see something I'd want

place, they will feel different. You could say that the fiberglass boat moves *on* the water, while a wooden boat moves *through* the water.

In the glass boat, the center of gravity is a lot higher, and that means there's more motion, and that wears you out quicker. You spend a lot more energy to keep your balance all day long. Fellas that have been fishing in fiberglass hulls find that their knees and their hips play out. They say that fiberglass is cold and dead and doesn't give.

But the wooden boat is a better sea boat and has a steadier motion because the center of gravity is lower. That means the boat will have less tendency to roll. And with wood, you're standing on something that had life once. It's more alive,

to change in the next one.

Even if it was one of my own hulls that was molded in glass, I'd have a problem finishing it off, because there would be things I would want to change, and in a glass hull I couldn't. I could only build that one exact same hull over and over again. I'd be stuck with it.

Of course, you can change the way it's finished off, but that's not enough. What keeps my interest is to be able to think about how to make it different. When you build in wood, every boat's a new boat to build. The next one's a new challenge. But if you've got that fiberglass mold, there'd be no challenge any more.

I'm too creative to be stuck with just one

design. Once I build a boat, I don't want to build that boat again. I want to build another one that's different and make it better. With wood, I *can* change each boat a little bit. If there are things that I see as I'm working on it that I want to do differently, I can make little changes as I go along.

There have been many times that Marion has seen me sitting at the kitchen table working over designs, making those corrections to the model. Then you have the opportunity to refine those designs again when they are laid out on the shop floor, and you can still make final changes during the construction of the boat itself. I'm always striving to get a better model, a better hull, better built.

For me, building a fiberglass hull isn't such a pleasant experience, either. I never liked the smell of the resin. But it *is* pleasant to steam timbers, bend them in, and plank a boat up. You get the smell of the steam and the wood. Even when you're getting out the plank, the shavings smell good. It's hard work, but it's fun planing those planks, seeing the shavings curling up off the long jointer planes, cutting the bevels, clamping them on, and fitting them. And you can see the boat taking shape.

Working with wood is like sculpture. Every piece of wood you've got to shape with your hand, and every fastener you've got to put in place by hand. You work hard, but there's a lot of satisfaction once it's done.

If I had just built fiberglass hulls and put them out for somebody else to finish, I'd have made a lot more money. But I didn't want to build a hull and let somebody else finish it. I had spent all those years learning to build wooden boats and perfecting my skills and perfecting my models, my designs, and I thought, "What's the point if I give it up?"

I thought, boats have been evolving this way for thousands of years in wood. If everybody just stopped building in wood, the art of building a boat would soon be lost.

CHAPTER *Twenty-two*

A BOATBUILDER'S LAMENT

Boatbuilding's always been a risky business. You're always working on a shoestring, and it's an art, and you're always trying to do your best, trying to improve. But I probably wouldn't encourage anybody to go into the business of building wooden lobster boats today.

You might be able to make a go of it if you had a one-man or a two-man shop, in partnership, and could keep your overhead down. There's a lot of overhead in boatbuilding. If I pay someone, hypothetically, a dollar an hour, I've got to charge three dollars an hour to cover everything like Social Security and unemployment insurance and health benefits. Then there's the shop overhead like the lights, taxes, truck, office,

and all those expenses. One or two men building a boat wouldn't have all that.

One of the challenges we face as builders is a decline in the suppliers of traditional hardware and lumber for boats. There are certain things you want—like stuffing boxes or port lights—that you used to be able to get easily. You could go to the hardware or marine-supply store and buy them right off the shelf. Now you have to order them special. It takes a long time, and sometimes you can't get them at all.

The quality of bronze hardware isn't top-notch like it used to be years ago, either. A lot of the big manufacturers have gone out of business or left the country. It's frustrating in building a traditional boat that a lot of the proper hardware is no longer made. Sometimes you have to make the pattern for a piece, go to a foundry, and have it cast. Getting something cast out of bronze in this country isn't easy. Up in Randolph there used to be a nice foundry that cast bronze fittings for me. They'd also cast lead keels. But they've gone out of business. The environmental regulations became so strict they couldn't continue, even though they had been in business for over a hundred years.

It's also hard to get finished lumber to work with. When I first started building, there were mills that knew how to cut wood for boats and specialized in it. You could call and give them an order, and they knew exactly what you wanted. It would come the finished size, and you could use it for a lobster boat just as it was delivered. If I was going to do a pleasure boat and wanted things fancy, I would have to order the wood a little bigger so I could plane it myself. But building a lobster boat you could get everything finished size, right from the mill.

These days, you have to scout around for lumber, and it's hard to find somebody that understands what you want. You have to educate the mill owners. Like about sawing planks. If you've got a log that has a sweep—a curve—to it, you want to save the sweep in the plank you cut. But most of the sawmills today will just lay a nice, crooked log down flat and get two straight boards out of it when they could have ended up with six good planks that had a sweep.

Many of the old mills have gone out of busi-ness. The ones that are left generally can saw the lumber pretty accurately, but then they don't usu-ally want to plane things. They just pull the wood off the saw and that's it. You have to take that rough-sawed lumber and send it somewhere else that's got the capacity to plane big stuff. Usually that's too time-consuming, so you just plane it and smooth it up yourself. That's something we didn't have to do years ago. It makes more work in the shop, so it takes more time to build the boat.

Nowadays, it's even a hard job to find people to cut logs for boat wood. I mean the men that go into the woods to select the trees. There are plenty of trees, but there are not many now that know which ones to look for and how to cut them.

Years ago, farmers usually had a woodlot on their land. There'd be oak trees growing, and they'd go in the woods in the wintertime and cut those oaks and use their horses or oxen to pull them out. They could go in and cut just one tree and haul it out. Nowadays, you've got to go in with a skidder, you've got to cut a big road, and—in order to make it pay—you've got to cut a num-ber of trees. Farmers now don't bother to cut their trees because it doesn't pay, and they don't have the horses and oxen. In order to get a spe-cial tree now, you've got to hunt for somebody that will go find it and cut it. That makes a dif-ference in boatbuilding today.

The workforce has changed, too. Up until the 1970s, the people who worked in boatyards were mostly local men who had a long connection with boats, either by fishing or whatever. But during the '70s, there was a renewed interest in traditional methods, and we began to see younger people that were interested in learning to build boats. They'd work here for a few years, and then they'd leave.

I've had a lot of the students from the boat school up in Washington County come down here and work for their required eight weeks. They still do, about every year. But it's a hard job for those young people. If they haven't grown up with boats, they've missed something. And today, the child-labor laws won't allow you to work in a boatyard until you're sixteen years old. Nevertheless, if someone today was really interested in building, I'd tell them to go to boat school. I would have if there had been one at the time.

Then again, I might tell them to just start in and build something, or to work at something else to get by, and save enough money to build a boat. If a fella does that, somebody'll see his work and want something else, and gradually he'll build up a business. It takes the right person, but if you want to learn how and build a boat, you can do it.

CHAPTER *Twenty-three*

OUR ADVENTURE IN SARDINIA

Mrs. Anne Franchetti lives on the island of Sardinia, off the coast of Italy, but she's really a citizen of Tremont, on Mount Desert Island.

I've known her since I was eighteen years old. Her mother was Mrs. Milliken, and Mrs. Montgomery was her aunt. Of course, those ladies were young and had small children when I worked on their boats for them.

In 1995, we built a twenty-one-foot sailboat for Mrs. Franchetti that was based on the lines of the nineteen-footer I came up with in 1985. We changed the design a little bit and made the transom elliptical. It has a couple of berths in the cabin and a little Yanmar two-cylinder diesel for an engine. The name of that boat is the *Ralph W. Stanley.*

Years before, Mrs. Franchetti had talked about having Steve Spurling and me go over and build a boat for her in Sardinia. But that didn't come to pass. Then she had talked about having a boat to use over here, at Pretty Marsh. But, she considered the time she spent at Pretty Marsh and the time she was at Sardinia, where she had people that could use it. She said it would be better to send the boat over there.

When we built that twenty-one-footer, she'd had one of her fellas over here, and we'd been showing him how to sail in another boat, a

Trial run of the Ralph W. Stanley *in Maine.*

Hauling her out for shipment.

nineteen-footer. But when it came time to ship the boat to Sardinia, Mrs. Franchetti wanted me to go over with Marion and be there when it was launched–to help rig it and get it going.

We shipped the nineteen-footer in February 1996, and then Marion and I went over the next month. I had never flown before, and I didn't care about airplanes, especially across the ocean. Marion and I talked about maybe sending the boat across and going with it on a freighter. But there was no ship that would take the boat and passengers, too, so that was out. It ended up that we had to fly. I told Marion I'd probably die if I had to fly, but I did it anyway.

We needed passports, and we had to go to Bangor to get our pictures taken. There was only one place that could do that. The passports finally came through, but they took a while.

It was on the tenth of March that we left Bangor, just before dark. We flew to Boston and had to wait there a while to get on the plane for Sardinia. We went first class, so we waited in a special waiting area, and we got on the plane all right. We were all night long flying across. There was a moon out most all night, but if you looked down you couldn't see much of anything except clouds. I slept some.

We got over to Rome, and Mrs. Franchetti had a relative there to meet us. That lady could speak English, and she got us a taxi. It seemed as if we were forever getting to Mrs. Franchetti's apartment. It was quite an adventure riding around Rome with those little narrow streets and cars going here, there, and everywhere.

The apartment was way up on the top floor of this building that her son owned, quite close to the Spanish Steps. It was mid-forenoon when we got there, and we had a little nap. Then a fella that took care of her apartment and was a handyman, a cook, and everything, cooked us something for supper that night, and we were all set.

Loading her into the shipping container.

Into the water again in Sardinia

We were in Rome five days because of the weather, waiting to get to Sardinia. It was rainy and damp, but we were pretty comfortable in Rome. Mrs. Franchetti's son took us around the city in his car, and this fella that worked for her took us out on foot to the stores and up to a little park. Marion wanted to bring him home with us. He came from the island of Mauritius in the Indian Ocean. He could speak English fairly well, and of course he spoke Italian. He was a nice fella.

After five days, we went on another plane to Sardinia. It only took us about a half-hour to fly across. When we finally got over to the island, there had been a terrible rainstorm, and it had washed out the road that went to her place. So we had to go in one car from the airport to the washout, and then we had to walk across it with all our baggage and get in another car for the rest of the way.

Sardinia is the largest island in the Mediterranean, and it would take you quite a while to go all the way around it. We saw the city of Olbia, and that's quite a big place with a lot of people. The weather was cool and chilly, but it was still better than Maine in March.

We'd have lunch at the house, and one day they roasted a goat. It was on a spit all day long in a walk-in fireplace, and it was pretty darn good. And, of course, we ate a lot of spaghetti.

We were there in Sardinia for five days, and we got the boat rigged and put some sails on her. Then we went back to Rome and spent the night in the apartment. The next morning we got on a plane and came home. When we got to Boston we caught the flight for Bangor, and in the evening Tim and Nadine met us there and brought us home.

I guess Marion liked the trip, but I sure don't like to fly. But, I figured I was sixty-seven years old and I had lived long enough, so I might as well go. I don't care about flying ever again.

CHAPTER *Twenty-four*

FIDDLING FOR FUN

Besides boatbuilding, one of my main interests is music. I've learned how to play the fiddle, I can play the banjo a little bit, and I can play chords on the piano in certain keys.

I never had any lessons, but my grandmother was musical. Way back when I was a kid, she had a fiddle, and she could play a few little tunes. I was fascinated by it. I used to get her to dig it out now and then and play something.

Then when I was going to school up in Houlton, there was a fella there who could play. So, when I came home I dug out that old fiddle to see if I could do anything with it. I kept fooling around, and I got so I could pick out a few tunes. Then my mother got me a fiddle of my own, and I learned how to play a few more tunes.

When I was in the hospital with tuberculosis, I couldn't have my fiddle for six or seven months. But after I'd had my lung operation and got up to the sanatorium in Fairfield, they let me have a fiddle there. There was another fella who had a guitar, and we used to get together and play. Then there was a barber who came in from Waterville, and he played my fiddle for us.

The more I heard the music, the more excited I got. I came home and wanted to *build* a fiddle. I got some books that told how to do it and I built one and I played that. Later on, I bought another fiddle that was in pieces and got interested in repairing old violins. I've got five or six

The Country Strummers: Floyd Farley, Ruth Grierson, me, and Fred Black.

now, but the one I fixed is the only one that I play.

At one time, we had a little group called the Western Mountain Boys, and we used to play at the Knights of Pythias Lodge. Different people would come in and sing and play guitars or harmonicas. It was an impromptu thing, and you never knew who was going to play, because different ones would come and go, and the group kept changing. But it went over good. People came from everywhere to hear us play.

We did this every other week, and we had a good time. We played old-fashioned country tunes and some from back in the Civil War days. Somebody'd come along and sing, and I could generally follow them with the fiddle. We had a lot of fun. We played at the Lodge one winter and they took donations—they had a fishbowl to put money in—and they did pretty well. I think they collected $400 that winter, and it was enough to shingle the roof.

Then there were a few in the group that

Fiddling for fun, with Wilbur Wolf playing the piano in my living room.
(Portraits of our four children are on the wall behind.)

thought, "Gee, we're pretty good. We ought to get paid for this." So they started charging. But they'd have arguments, and it wouldn't go good. As long as everybody played for free it was fine.

After that faded out, a bunch of us started going down to Ruth Grierson's to play. The nucleus of it was Fred Black, Floyd Farley, Ruth, and myself. Sometimes Richard played the wash-tub base with us, sometimes Skip Farley did, and sometimes Ruth's son Scott did. When Ruth first came to town, we had her down here to my house one night, and she played my piano. Then we started meeting down at her house about every

Saturday night. We got together a little group that we called the Country Strummers. We played for weddings, fraternal lodges, and senior-citizen events.

We had that little group for a number of years, and it was fun while it lasted. Once we stopped performing as a group, Fred Black and Buddy Seavey and I would meet up in Fred's house, and sometimes other people would join in. Ruth and I still get together to play once in a while, and my friend Wilbur Wolf and I do, too. He plays the piano, and we have a good time.

Ralph's Hornpipe

Ralph's playing, 4 May 2003

Ralph Stanley

Reel

Ralph's Jig

Ralph's playing, 4 May 2003

Ralph Stanley

Jig

CHAPTER *Twenty-five*

TRACING MY ANCESTRY

Both sides of my family have been here on Mount Desert Island since the 1760s. I'm descended from about twenty of the earliest settlers. I think I've been quite lucky to be able to live and work as a man where I played as a boy and where my ancestors have been for generations.

I've always been interested in family history, and I got that mostly from my grandmother, Celestia Dix Robinson. I always enjoyed the stories she used to tell about the family. I always asked her about the old people and what they did. Of course, there were always boats and local history tied into it, too.

I've done quite a bit of research into my fam-

ily tree, and with a lot of the lines I can go back to my immigrant ancestors. Most of them came from England. On my father's side, I can trace the Boynton line to 1606 in England. I can follow the Dix line back on my mother's side, and a number of those ancestors were sea captains.

William Dix, who was my grandmother's great-grandfather was here on Mount Desert Island quite early—by 1800 or before. The Dixes settled on the west side of the Island over in Goose Cove on Dix Point. There's still a cemetery that some of my ancestors are buried in, but the alders are all grown up. Those Dixes were relatives of the famous social reformer Dorothea Dix of Hampden, Maine.

My grandmother's mother was Emily Bartlett, and her father was John Dix. Emily Bartlett's father was Abraham Bartlett, and her mother was Jerusha Mayo. Jerusha was a Mayflower descendent, in the line of Elder William Brewster.

Abraham Bartlett was a captain of vessels. His father was Christopher Bartlett, the original settler of Bartlett's Island, and his mother was Freelove Razee. They came up from Connecticut in 1763, before the Revolutionary War, but I believe they originated in Massachusetts on the Merrimac River, just above Newburyport.

My great-grandfather John Dix was a sea captain, and my grandmother always said that he was once shipwrecked, but she didn't know where. She was just a little girl at the time, and she couldn't remember much about it. She thought it might have been "on the Jersey coast." Anyway, he lost his ship, and it took him two years to get home. The story went that he had traded one vessel for another one at Blue Hill, and she almost sank before he got her home to Bartlett's Island across the bay. She'd been down in the Caribbean and hadn't been coppered, so she was worm-eaten. Even though she was a fairly new vessel, they had to fix her up before they could use her.

I'm not sure whether this was the same ship he lost or not, but I've got a picture of a brig that was drawn by Fred W. Dix, who was lost at sea in 1886 and who was some kind of cousin to my great-grandfather. It's just a picture on a piece of lined paper, hand colored. On the back it says "Built in New Haven, 1882," and it says *Carrie F. Dix* on the flag.

Now, Carrie F. Dix was my grandmother's sister. Carrie married Dr. Joseph Dana Phillips, but she died in childbirth. Dr. Phillips sent my grandmother and their other sister, Vienna, to school at Coburn Classical Institute in Waterville. Then my grandmother taught school on Tinker's Island for a time, and she also taught on Bartlett's Island, where she lived.

On the back of this picture of the brig it also says, "First trip to Faroe Isles and then to a place in Norway." After that, the writing fades out, and the rest of it is illegible. I've tried using a black light to read it, but I can't make it out. It says something about some port in Spain, so John Dix was probably bound down through the English Channel.

Whether he was wrecked on the Channel Isles and spent some time on the island of Jersey, I don't know. If the ship had been lost off *New* Jersey, it wouldn't have taken him two years to get home. I do know that the whole crew was rescued by breeches buoy. But I bet my great-grandfather *was* shipwrecked on the Channel Isles, and he might have had to stay on the island of Jersey.

Now, he might have been hurt or might have had a nervous breakdown over losing that vessel, because it took him two years to recover enough to get home. He had no money. When he got back to Maine, his spirit was broken and he never went to sea again. He had to run that little farm on Bartlett's Island, and his family was

Brig   C.F.D.   Painted By   Fred. W. Dix   1882

The Carrie F. Dix

very poor. When his daughter Emily Bartlett died, John Dix came off the island and lived in Southwest Harbor with another daughter, Vienna Lawler. When he died, they had Emily's body brought over and buried with his, down at Mount Height Cemetery.

I can remember asking my grandmother about Bartlett's Island and looking over the stuff my great-grandfather A. J. Robinson had in his sea chest. There were old navigation books and coast pilots and lists of merchant vessels. I stud-

ied them. I've still got a caulking iron that A. J. Robinson had in his sea chest. I've used it a lot, and my son Richard uses it now.

Another branch of my mother's family—the Clarks—were quite enterprising people, too. When my great-great-grandfather Seth Clark built his house here on Clark Point in 1847, it was a Cape. But by the 1870s, most every house in Southwest took in summer boarders, and he had an upper story added so that he could accommodate more visitors.

Seth and his brother, Deacon Henry H. Clark, built the steamboat wharf in Southwest Harbor back in 1853. The Clarks ran that wharf for three generations until the steamboat service disappeared. Deacon Clark also had a brickyard here on the shore. They dug the clay to make bricks right down the street from where my house is. Those bricks were used as ballast when a schooner would sail away empty on their way to pick up a cargo. Then they could always sell the bricks when they got there. If they had taken rocks, they'd have had to throw them away.

Deacon Henry Clark also started taking people into his house as guests for the summer. More and more summer people came, and his house kept getting bigger and bigger. Finally it blossomed into the Island House. Bar Harbor was bustling with more activity, but I think the Island House right down here on Clark Point Road was the first summer hotel on Mount Desert Island. Deacon Clark even built an annex to it called the Pemetic, farther up on the hill.

Nathan Clark, the father of Seth and Henry, had mills at the dam on Norwood's Cove. He also owned land up towards Western Mountain, where they had a lumber camp. That was virgin forest then. Men would go in and stay all winter in that camp and cut logs. They'd bring them out on sleds in the wintertime, on the snow, and land them on the ice in the mill pond. It was a tide mill, and in the spring when the ice melted, they'd saw those logs into lumber. They also had a grist mill there.

Nathan had several sons and they probably all went to sea at one time or another. That was the thing to do. Every young man went to sea, and I think Nathan went also, because they called him Captain Nathan Clark. His sons eventually owned their own vessels, and they were engaged in carrying lumber.

My great-grandmother's sister, Grace Clark, married a sea captain named Jesse Pease. After he retired, they built the Claremont Hotel, and after he died she ran it by herself. Then she decided she wanted to sell it, and Dr. Phillips bought it. That eased up her responsibility, but Grace ran that hotel for him for years.

There are some interesting stories on my father's side, too. He was born on Great Cranberry Island in 1900. His father was Arno, and his mother was Mabel. She was a Stanley, too. Her father was Robert Stanley, and her mother was Phoebe Jane Gilley, who was descended from Jacob Lurvey and Hannah Boynton.

I'm descended twice from Jacob Lurvey through his two daughters. He came to Mount Desert Island in the 1790s. His wife's father, Enoch Boynton, was a farmer in Byfield, Massachusetts, and at the age of six Jacob was indentured to Enoch to earn his keep. In return, Enoch was supposed to feed him and clothe him and teach him to read and write. He did that somewhat, but Enoch couldn't read and write very well, himself. His wife could, though.

I've seen Jacob Lurvey's articles of indenture, and they were supposedly signed by his mother. But the woman he called his mother was different than the woman who signed the articles. That was Hannah Grimes. She was the widow of Manzel Rawl, and then she married William Nathaniel Hadlock. So she'd either been married to Samuel Lurvey first, or Jacob was an illegitimate child, in which case they might have indentured him to make sure he had a place. I haven't been able to find out.

In any event, Jacob grew up on that farm in Massachusetts, and when he was fifteen the Revolutionary War came along. He wanted to serve, but he couldn't because he was indentured. The only way he could do it was if Enoch Boynton went, too. So Enoch Boynton did go. They both served in the war, and they were at Valley Forge.

The story has come down through the family that Jacob was the young soldier with the bleeding, frostbitten feet—the one that George Washington gave his boots to. I've always thought this story has been told about every soldier at Valley Forge, but I found somebody in the family that hadn't been associated with the Lurveys here for years and years. The same story came down to him, too. So it may have been true.

After the war, Jacob was relieved of his indenture for his service, and he went to sea. He made several foreign voyages and he was ship-

With six of my sisters: Mary (front left), Ruth, Phoebe, Myrna, Esther, and Nancy (front right).

wrecked. They thought he was lost. But somehow or other he swam to a ledge and then to another ledge, and finally he was rescued and got home. After that, he married Hannah Boynton, who was Enoch Boynton's youngest daughter, a girl Jacob had grown up with.

They had five children in Massachusetts before they moved to Maine. He came here originally in the summer, on a fishing trip, and bought land from Joseph Bunker "from the mountain to the ocean" up at Norwood's Cove. He built a log cabin there, then he went back to Newburyport and picked up his family. His father-in-law came with him and stayed that first winter. They'd grown vegetables to bring with them, and they settled in for the winter.

One of Jacob's descendants was my great-grandfather Enoch Boynton Stanley. They called him "Enoch B.," and his wife was Caroline

Guptill. She came from Winter Harbor to Cranberry Island as a young woman to teach school. That's where she married Enoch B. He owned five or six fishing schooners, and the last one was the *S.L. Foster*, which he used for mackerel seining.

I don't think that anybody in the family aside from Enoch B. did much boatbuilding. My grandfather's brother, Uncle Lew Stanley, told me that the main part of their house wasn't finished off and that they lived in the ell. He said his father, Enoch B., built two or three boats in the other part of the house. They were small open sailboats, about sixteen to eighteen feet long, and they'd use them to gillnet herring down in the gut between Little Cranberry Island and Great Cranberry Island. The Gloucester schooners would come in and buy this herring for bait. I think they also "torched" herring out in the gut, using the light to attract the fish at night.

The Stanleys have been fishermen for a long time. We think they first came to this area of Maine from Marblehead, Massachusetts, around 1755. About that time, the French were seizing Colonial fishing vessels on the Grand Banks, and I think the Stanleys switched their fishing operation up to the Maine coast just to stay away from the French raiders.

They must have looked for grounds where they wouldn't be bothered. In those days, they would have fished here in Maine during the summer, dried their fish, and then carried them back to Marblehead, where they lived for the winter.

Gradually they came here and stayed year round, and by 1763 they were pretty well settled here on the Cranberry Islands.

There were two brothers there, Sans and John. My father's mother was descended from John, who settled on Islesford, on *Little Cranberry Island*. My father's father was descended directly from Sans on *Great Cranberry Island*. So I'm descended from both of them, and I'm descended from one of them twice.

Sans was lost at sea when he was twenty-six years old, and one of the first land grants in this area was to his wife, Widow Margaret Stanley. She was deeded a hundred acres on Great Cranberry Island, including the Fish Point and half of Dead Man's Point. Her maiden name was Homan, and there's a Homan's Beach in Marblehead. Eventually she went back there, and she died and is buried there.

John and his wife had children before they came up here. She was French, and I don't know whether she was one of the Acadians that were driven out of Nova Scotia or one of the French Huguenots that came to Marblehead. I haven't been able to trace her much. Her name was Margaretta LeCroix. I've got an old journal from Marblehead, two volumes of it about the time just before the Revolutionary War, and this name is mentioned there. On Little Cranberry Island she started a tradition of erecting a Maypole, and now the place is still called Maypole Point.

As far as we can tell, we're not related to the Stanley Steamer family. I think they came across

With my sisters Irene, Ruth, and Nancy, and my wife, Marion.

at a later date. Maybe back in England the two lines were related; it's hard to tell. I'm not sure where our branch of Stanleys came from in England, but the word is that they were chased out of the country for stealing sheep. Near as I can determine, my side of the family came to Marblehead in the 1640s or 1650s.

In those days, Marblehead was a tough town. It was an embarrassment to Salem, next door, because Salem was pious and Puritan. All the dregs of society ended up in Marblehead, but the Salem people had to put up with them because they were all fishermen, and Salem needed the fish. They just closed the town gate to keep the people from Marblehead out.

They also used the gate to keep out people that were sick. There were big typhoid scares, even into the 1700s, just before the Revolutionary War. They had a smokehouse near the gate, and if they suspected that you were contaminated with typhoid or diphtheria, you had to sit in there until the germs were supposedly killed. That was the way the story went, and it has been passed down through the generations.

CHAPTER *Twenty-six*

MY INTEREST IN LOCAL HISTORY

I can remember even as a little boy, maybe five years old, asking my grandmother how things were done years and years ago. I kept quizzing her about what happened when she was a girl on Bartlett's Island, and she told me a lot. I wish she'd told me even more.

I used to like to listen to my other relatives tell stories, too. My grandmother had a cousin who came to visit us now and then, and he'd usually arrive unannounced. His name was Lute Dix, and he was an interesting old fella. He was tall and thin, and he had a big mustache. He was deafer than a post, and he talked in a monotone.

Lute lived with his daughter and her husband, and he just about drove them crazy. They would drop him off on the sidewalk in front of my grandmother's house, and they wouldn't even come in. Of course, they knew we wouldn't turn him away.

But if you could get him started on something like schooners, he'd talk steady.

Artemus Richardson was another relative who used to tell me stories about the old times. He enjoyed telling these old stories, and I liked to listen to them. When I started building boats, he used to come down and visit me, or I'd see him up in the filling station uptown. There'd be a crowd of men gathered in the evening to talk and swap stories, and Artemus was always there.

There was no television in those days, so the old fellas used to listen to the six o'clock news on the radio. After supper, they'd walk uptown and stop in at the filling station. That's what they did for entertainment. They had to get out of the house. They'd talk for an hour or so and then go back home.

Another place where these fellas used to tell

stories was down at the fish wharf or at the fish market in the afternoon. Their work would be done, and they'd be waiting for the boats to come in, and all the workers on the wharf would gather to talk. I used to walk down there after school and hang around the fish wharf for a while until the boats came in.

They used to gather in the barbershop, too. There were actually two in town, and they were open every night till at least eight o'clock. The fellas used to gather there whether or not they needed a haircut or a shave.

One of the men I used to see was Chris Lawler. He was related to me through his mother, who was a Robinson. She was some kind of cousin to my grandfather, maybe once or twice removed. And his father's brother was married to my grandmother's sister, Vienna. Chris used to be there at the gas station or the barbershop, and he'd tell about things that had happened years ago. If he didn't have a true story, he'd make up a wonderful one right off the top of his head. He could make up stories just as fast as he could talk.

Chris was older than I was. He was probably born in 1890, and he was really quite smart. He could speak French, and if he'd gone to school, he could have done a lot more. But he just had a team of horses that he worked, and it's all he did. He used to get in messes sometimes and get me to go help him out. One time when I had just got my first boat built, Chris came by early one morning, and he says, "Ralph, can't you take your boat and go help me?"

He'd cut a bunch of pilings for Southwest Boat, and he had piled them down on his shore. His sons were supposed to tie them off there, but they forgot. Chris woke up the next morning, and these pilings were drifting off, one right after another, out by King's Point, the whole length of the harbor.

I said "Okay." We went down to Charlie Rich's dock, and the lobster warden was there. He says to Chris, "What are *you* doing down here?"

"Oh, we're going lobstering," Chris says. "We haven't got any traps, but we'll find plenty out there!"

Of course, the lobster warden knew that Chris was just pulling his leg. Anyway, we got in the boat and went out, and there were those pilings, drifting out of the harbor. We got them rounded up and towed them back in to Southwest Boat.

One winter when I was in my early twenties, Chris had sent his son and another guy to the top of Long Hill with the horses to get out some logs that they'd been cutting. It had to be done that day because Arnold Allen was coming after the wood the next morning. But along about the middle of the afternoon, they got bored with working and decided to go up to the beer parlor for a drink. When it came six o'clock, they were still there, and the horses were still over in the woods.

So, Chris came and got me. He says, "Can't you go help me?"

There was snow on the ground and it was after supper and it was dark, but I said, "Yeah, I guess so."

He says, "Meet me down to the barn in ten

minutes." It was "meet me in ten minutes" every time he'd come up. So I got ready and went down in my truck, and we drove over.

It was darker than the devil in those woods, and it was cold. The horses were standing there in harness and they'd gone to sleep and they didn't want to move. Now, Chris had bought these horses from the Great Northern Paper Company, and they'd always been run by Frenchmen, so he started talking French to them. They began stamping their feet and shaking themselves and snorting a little bit and woke up.

We led the horses to where Chris wanted the logs dropped off, and he says, "Now you just stand here. I'll go up and hook the logs on, and the horses will bring them down. All you've got to do is stand here and unhook them."

"Well," I said, "how am I going to stop them?"

"Oh! You haven't got to stop them," he says. "The horses know when to stop, and they'll slack the chain so you can unhook it."

Chris went up the hill to hook the logs on and, sure enough, I could hear the horses coming down, dragging the logs through the snow. When they got right to where I was standing, they stopped. Then they backed up and slacked the chain. There was just a grab hook on the end of it, and all I had to do was unfasten it. The *minute* I got it unhooked, away the horses went, back up for another load.

"Well," I thought, "I've got to be awfully careful. If I ever fumble that chain and my fingers are still in there, the team is apt to think I've got it

unhooked, and they'll take off." So, I *was* awful careful, and we did this six or eight times. Everything went fine. Finally, though, one load came down and the chain was jammed and I fumbled it. There was ice and dirt in the hook, and I couldn't get it clear.

My fingers were in under the chain, and I thought "Oh, my God, what'll I do? They're going to start." But the horses never budged a bit. They stood right there. I had to work quite a while to get that chain off, but finally I got it unhooked, and they knew. Away they went!

Those horses really enjoyed doing that job. It was like a dog chasing a stick and bringing it back. The team knew just what to do, and they liked doing it.

Chris had a little hovel to put the horses away in after we finished up, and then I brought him back to his regular barn. As we were walking up the road, he says, "Oh, Ralph, don't you like this kind of weather—that nice, crisp air and the snow crunching under your feet? It's wonderful, isn't it?"

There were quite a few people like that around town back then, and I got an awful lot from those old fellas telling what happened years ago. It was local history that I was interested in. But by the time I got married, most everybody had a TV, and the men didn't come out after supper. So we lost all that. Those old fellas were gone, anyway, and nobody carried it on.

I guess I'm the one who's telling the stories now, and in recent years, I've been asked to do quite a few lectures about history. Back when I was going to high school I'd had a class in public speaking. I dreaded it at the time. I thought, "I'll never get up and talk in front of a crowd anyway." But I got through the class, and years later, when I was asked to get up and do a lecture, it didn't bother me a bit. Now I've done quite a few.

I've given talks on local history at the Northeast Harbor Library and the Southwest Harbor Library. I'm on the library board here in Southwest, and that's another thing I've got to keep going. I'll probably be on that forever. These boards need people that are native to the area. I've also given a number of talks about the history of shipbuilding on Mount Desert Island. I'm related to so many people here that my family history always ties into it somehow.

Another way that I'm able to pursue this interest is through the different local historical societies. I've been vice president and a director of the Tremont Historical Society, and I'm a member of the Cranberry Island Historical Society and the Deer Isle Historical Society. I've also been a director of the Islesford Historical Society.

I've spoken on marine history at the Maine Maritime Museum at Bath and the Penobscot Marine Museum in Searsport. In 1999 I was named a director of the Penobscot Marine Museum.

I really like to do research. That's why the Mount Desert Historical Society has named their research room for me. They've rebuilt the old schoolhouse in a village that used to be known as the Sound, in the town of Mount Desert, as a home for all their records. I've been involved with that group for thirty years as a member, as vice president, and as president.

There's also an interesting project that I've been working on with Mary Jones of the Mount Desert Island Historical Society. She got a grant to study and record all the houses in Southwest Harbor that are over fifty years old. Mary took pictures and interviewed the people who now live in them. I told her about the people who lived in them in the past.

When we started getting information on all these old houses, we thought it would be nice to present this to the public, to let them know what we were doing. So we decided to put on a little program, and we picked out fifteen houses that were historically significant to the town.

The first time we made this presentation, we showed old pictures of the houses, and then we showed new pictures of the houses. We told how they were built and who lived in them. That first program lasted an hour or so, and it went over good. We did it over again at the Claremont Hotel, and we still had an overflowing crowd. That shows people are interested in the houses and the history of the town. Bob Vila found out about the work we were doing and did a feature on us for his "Restore America" program on cable TV.

Mary Jones and I have tried to make people in the community aware of the buildings that are important to the character of this town and we've encouraged their preservation. It would be nice if Southwest could stay the same, but you can't stop change.

CHAPTER
Twenty-seven

THE NATIONAL HERITAGE FELLOWSHIP

In the fall of 1998, a man named David Taylor, who worked in the Library of Congress, called me up to talk about nominating me for the National Heritage Fellowships.

Later he interviewed me up here in Southwest, and a lady came and took photographs of me and gathered up all my old pictures of the boats that I had built. Then away they went, and they said they wouldn't know the outcome until spring.

In June I got a call from David Taylor saying that I'd won. A few days later, Dan Sheehy, who was then the director of folk and traditional arts for the National Endowment for the Arts, called to confirm it. They'd pay my way down there to

Washington and pay for Marion to go with me. They'd put us up in a hotel and cart me around to whatever event I had to go to.

I wanted to call up and say, "What'll I wear? I've got a nice pair of coveralls, and I can bring along an adze to hold onto." I figured I'd have to dress up in a suit and a tie for the presentation, but I hoped I wouldn't have to wear a tuxedo. They would have had to rent me one, and they would have had to put it on me, probably.

Anyway, on Saturday morning the twenty-fifth of September, we drove to Bangor and got on the Concord Trailways bus. That took us to South Station in Boston. Then we got on the Amtrak train and went to Washington, D.C. We got there

Shaping the keel of Freedom *with an adze.*

about 11:30 that night. The National Endowment people met us there and took us to our hotel.

On Sunday we had a free day, and Hugh Dwelley came in. He's president of the Islesford Historical Society on Cranberry Island, and he lives in Fairfax, Virginia, just outside Washington. He and his wife, Shirley, drove us around the city, and then we went to Alexandria, Virginia, and looked over the waterfront there.

That's where my great-grandfather A. J. Robinson was with his schooner when his daughter died in Portland in the 1890s. He had to come home for the funeral, so he left his vessel in Alexandria and came home by steamboat. The

waterfront had changed since then, of course. It's not a working waterfront any more. You don't see any schooners, and there's not even a dock to tie up to.

We went on to George Washington's home at Mount Vernon and looked that all over and had lunch there. Both Hugh and I descend from Jacob Lurvey, and with the family legend about George Washington's boots, there was some personal significance to the place. I wish we still had those boots, but Jacob probably didn't keep them.

In the morning, I got together with Bob Holt, who's a fiddler and was one of the other Fellowship recipients, and we played a few tunes. He likes the same ones I do, only he's a much better fiddler than I am, and he adds a little bit more to them.

From 1:30 to 3:30 that afternoon, we were at the Carlisle Suites and had rehearsals for the big performance, where each of the recipients was to get up on stage and demonstrate their skill or be interviewed. The performance itself was to be held two days later at the Lisner Auditorium on the campus of George Washington University.

On Tuesday morning we went to the Congressional Awards Ceremony in the Gold Room at the Rayburn building. That was when we got our big framed awards. Bill Ivey, the chairman of the National Endowment for the Arts, made the presentations. The First Lady, Hillary Clinton, came in later from some other event, and we all had to get up and do it over again with her. That's when we had our pictures taken. They got

Marion and me on the porch at Mount Vernon, wondering where those boots went.

one picture of Mrs. Clinton and me holding up the award and then another one with her on one side of me and Congressman John Baldacci, from Bangor, on the other.

That night, there was a banquet on the top floor of the State Department, in the Benjamin Franklin room. It was a big dinner, and each one of us got up and made some little talk.

The next day, our group attended a separate presentation ceremony for the winners of the National Medal of Arts and the National Humanities Medal. Stephen Spielberg got an award, and so did Garrison Keillor, Aretha Franklin, Norman Lear, Jim Lehrer, and others. They were on the stage, and we were in the audience—in the first and second rows. The President spoke and Mrs. Clinton spoke and they both presented these awards.

At that event "The President's Own" Marine Chamber Orchestra played. They had six or seven violins, three violas, one or two cellos, a big bass viol, and some various horns. That was good.

One woman played a violin that was strung up left-handed. That was interesting. I wish I could have talked with her about it. The orchestra played for quite a while. The program was a long time getting going, so they had quite a workout waiting for the President and First Lady. They, of course are always late. Mick Moloney, one of the other National Heritage Fellows, and his band played, too.

On Thursday we practiced all morning and half the afternoon, then we went back to the hotel to rest a while. At seven o'clock we all lined up as we went on stage in the big performance at the Lisner Auditorium. Then after they introduced us, we marched off. Of course, there was a lot of applause. We were interviewed one by one on stage. There were two "acts" to the ceremony. I was in the second one, and I was the next to the last person interviewed. When they introduced me, they showed a short section from a movie that was made about me building the *Endeavor*. It shows Tim taking a timber out of the steam box with his gloves on and Steve with gloves on passing it to me. And there I am—with bare hands—bending the frame in with the steam coming off of it. The audience thought that was something.

I had a half model of the *Hieronymus,* my first Friendship sloop, there on the stage, and they asked me questions. Nick Spitzer, a professor from the University of New Orleans and the host of the *American Routes* program on public radio, was doing the interviewing, and he asked me why the bottom of the boat was green. I told

him that was antifouling paint to keep the barnacles from growing. He also asked if I had sailed down to Washington. I told him no, that I came on a train. But mostly he asked things about the boats. And that was that. It didn't last for very long. Afterwards, they had a little party and then we all left and went back to the hotel. I did enjoy the ceremony. It was pretty good. I still can't believe I was there.

I'd never been to Washington before, although Marion had. It's quite a city, and there's so much to see. Everybody's well dressed, and there are a lot of smart people there. Marion and some of the other recipients' wives went to the Smithsonian Institution, and when they found out that I was there with the model of the *Hieronymus,* they called me up and wanted it. I told them they couldn't have that one because it belonged to Albie Neilson, but I said they could have one of my other models.

On Friday, we had to get up at four o'clock in the morning to get ready for the trip home. We left the hotel about five-fifteen for the train station and got on the train and away we went.

Somebody asked me later how I felt about this award, and I said I didn't know. I'm not doing anything different than any other boatbuilder I ever knew when I was a kid, and I don't know as it's as much. But I guess that I'm the one that's left, and I've kept with it and stuck with it. I guess that's the main thing.

I've always tried to stick to whatever I set out to do, and that may be one of the reasons why I got the National Heritage Fellowship Award.

With the First Lady and Congressman Baldacci at the National Heritage Fellowship presentation.

Because I stuck with building wooden boats. That's been my outlook all along. If something's worth doing, you've got to do it right, and you've got to stick with it to get it done.

Marion was quite happy about my getting the award. I brought back my ten-thousand-dollar check, but I only got to keep part of that because it was taxable. I guess it was quite an honor. I wish some of the people that helped me get started were around to see it—my mother and father, and my grandmother, especially. And some of my old schoolteachers.

Many people have helped me over the years, even if they didn't realize it. Some just tolerated what I was doing, like making a lot of noise caulking a boat in the shop. It must have bothered the neighbors, but they didn't complain. And people loaned me things. They'd come in and see that I needed some sort of a tool and if they had it they'd bring it up to me to use. There seemed to be more of that in those days than today.

But I had some people along the way that *really* helped me. I had a growing family, and it was a hard job, scratchin' to make ends meet. Stores gave me credit, and my suppliers gave me credit. They had faith in what I was doing, I guess. So it would have been nice for some of those people to know that I got this award.

CHAPTER *Twenty-eight*

A NEW LEASE ON LIFE

In the winter of 1999, I had been having this little pain in my left arm, a dull ache. I only felt it now and again, and just momentarily. It would last maybe a half a minute, and then it would go right away.

But on Thursday morning, the sixteenth of December 1999, I got up quite early, about five-thirty, and I was going to take a bath. I got the tub ready, and I was going to jump in when the arm started aching again, and this time the pain ran to my shoulder and down my chest. It was bad enough that I sat down and rested maybe ten minutes or so.

I got thinking that I should get that bath and eat some breakfast. Maybe then the pain would go away. But it didn't. The arm still ached. Around eight o'clock, after dropping her son off at school,

Betsey Holtzmann came in and she said, "Oh, you look terrible. What's the matter?"

I said, "Well, I don't feel very good. I'm going to call my doctor as soon as the office opens up."

I sat here at the house and waited, and the ache subsided, but Marion thought I had better call the doctor anyway. I got his nurse and she relayed the message. The doctor said to go right to the emergency room as soon as I could. I thought I might just as well get my son-in-law Tim to drive me up to St. Joseph's in Bangor, where my doctor's office is. That way, I'd be right there at the hospital, just in case.

By the time I got to Bangor an hour later, the pain was almost gone, and I felt kind of foolish going into the emergency room. I thought they'd just send me home, but they rushed me right in and did an electrocardiogram and an ultrasound. And they said, "It looks like you're having a heart attack."

They kept me right there until they could send me over to Eastern Maine Medical Center for heart catheterization. There the doctors found I had three major arteries plugged—besides the main artery. They said, "You should have a bypass operation just as soon as possible. We'd like to schedule it for the first of the week."

I told them, "Okay, let's go for it."

At seven o'clock in the morning on Tuesday, I was in the operating room at Eastern Maine. It was a quadruple bypass, and for the next two hours, they were repiping me and stitching me up. I was in the recovery room most all day, and that night they took me up to the intensive-care unit. I was there for a day, and then they took me to a regular room on the ward.

While I was still in intensive care, they had me standing up, and when I got up to the regular room they had me out walking around the nurses' station. I had no trouble at all doing that but, of course, I went slowly. The nurse went around with me, and she says, "Well, I guess you don't need me."

I didn't feel bad, but I was so full of dope that I was all befuddled. I couldn't read anything, and that was awful aggravating. I tried a story in a magazine, but I just couldn't concentrate. It was that way all the time I was in the hospital, because they were putting the pain pills to me. I came home the day after Christmas, but even then I was taking those pain pills every four hours. They wanted me

to because the more pain you have, the slower the heart is to heal. But I finally got off them.

Once I got home, I had to go out and walk every day. On January nineteenth, I went back for a checkup. Our daughter Marjorie took me up there. They did an electrocardiogram and took x-rays, and the doctors said everything was fine. So I asked, "How soon can I start driving?"

"Oh, you can drive home if you want to," the doctor said. But I had my chauffeur there, so I decided I'd take advantage of that.

They said I bounced back quicker than expected. But I went into the operation with a positive attitude. I didn't dread it or anything. I knew it had to be done, and I wanted to get it over with as quick as I could so I could get back to building boats.

And I had faith in the doctors at Eastern Maine. *U.S. News & World Report* had an article about the best hospitals in the country for my kind of an operation, and Eastern Maine was one of them. They've got two teams that are doing bypass surgery all the time.

If I had just gone to work December sixteenth, I might have had another heart attack and died. But I guess it wasn't my time, and I think somebody was looking after me. It's like the time I nearly died of pneumonia when I was thirteen years old. There was some reason for me to come back, but I don't know why. As I've gotten older, I've thought more about that experience. There's something beyond, I think, and maybe I haven't accomplished my mission yet. So I've got a few more years here, I guess.

CHAPTER *Twenty-nine*

THE SINKING OF *ENDEAVOR*

On the first day of the Friendship sloop race at Rockland in July 2001, my son Richard was sailing *Endeavor* with a crew that consisted of Reverend David and Mrs. Nancy Bell, Lorraine Strauss and her brother, Robert.

Marion and I were in the *Seven Girls* assisting the race committee, along with Leo Campbell, a member of the Friendship Sloop Society who had volunteered to help by operating a handheld radio. At the start of the race we were asked to go out to the buoys in the middle of Penobscot Bay to report on the weather. The water was quite choppy, and the wind was breezing up stronger all the time.

We'd been out there for a while when the committee asked us to go stand by *Salatia*, as she had broken her gaff and the crew was having a hard time getting things secured. It took us a while to catch up with her, and by the time we did they were on their way in. The other sloops had rounded their marks and were sailing close-hauled down the shore towards Owls Head. We were probably half a mile from the first boats, and the wind had really picked up, with heavy gusts. We could see *Endeavor* with one boat ahead of her, and something just didn't seem right.

Richard was in a good position to win the race and was sailing her hard, and he had dipped the coaming several times, taking some water

155

aboard each time. Unfortunately, the bilge pump had been turned off and he didn't realize it until he noticed water slopping in the bilge. Richard turned on the pump, but then a heavy gust hit them along with a big sea, putting her rail under again.

This time they lost their steerage, and the cockpit filled in a minute. I could see the boat slow down and heel way over. She righted, and then she went under.

When I saw her sails going down and the mast disappearing, I knew Richard was in trouble. I'd already headed for him by that time, and I opened up the *Seven Girls* to full speed. We were probably half a mile away at that point, and we tried to call for help on our hand-held radio as we headed for them. But we couldn't get an answer.

I knew it was up to us to pick them up if we could. I wished it was somebody else besides me, but I was there and I had to do it. My heart was pounding, and I really felt pretty tight in my chest. I'd had the heart attack and the quadruple bypass operation in '99, and only six months before the race I'd had a shunt put in. I was just hoping that my heart could take the stress and that I could get out there and help the *Endeavor's* crew.

Marion was really scared to think that they weren't all right. She kept asking, "Where are they? Where are they?"

I tried to steer for the spot where I last saw the mast, but it's hard to go directly to a place when there's nothing there. It was so choppy that I couldn't see anyone in the water, and we didn't know what we'd find when we got there. I was afraid that somebody might have been caught in the rigging and been pulled down with the boat.

It took about ten minutes to get to the crew, and I was quite close before I could see their heads in the water. It was a relief to find that everyone had gotten clear. I wanted to get them as quickly as possible but I didn't dare to rush right up. I didn't want to give them a washing with my wake and make it all the worse; they were getting washed enough with all the chop. I was also afraid I might hit them with the boat.

We tried to get Mrs. Bell aboard first. Marion and I were on each side of her, trying to pull her up into the *Seven Girls*. It's awfully hard to lift a person up over the side of a boat when it's rolling and pitching, and we couldn't do it by ourselves. We could only get her up so far, but we didn't dare let go.

I had a rope aboard with a loop spliced in the end, and I held this over the side for Mrs. Bell to put her foot into. But she couldn't manage that, so I had to reach over the side and put the loop on her foot. Then, with her pushing and our lifting and Leo reaching over her shoulder to get hold of her belt and pull, we got her aboard. She got bruised up pretty bad, but other than being black-and-blue she seemed to be fine, and she was glad to be alive.

Richard and Robert were holding onto the rail of the *Seven Girls*, and they were able to help Lorraine in over the side. Robert got in pretty much by himself. He was the youngest one in the crowd and had the most energy. Then Richard made it, but I still couldn't see David Bell, who was up under the bow at that point. When I could see where he was, we got him in, too. They all needed something warm to put around them, so Marion went below and got our sleeping bags, blankets, and an afghan we had on board.

I took some visual marks of our position, and after picking up the things that had floated clear—the engine box with its cover, the compass and its box, and some floorboards—we headed for Rockland Harbor. Since our bedding was all wet, we could not sleep on board *Seven Girls* that night, so we got a room in a hotel nearby. I watched the news at eleven on TV and thought I would go right asleep as I was quite tired. But my heart was still pounding, and I didn't close my eyes all night.

I probably should have gone to the hospital emergency room that night for a checkup, but I didn't, and the next day I was surprised that I was not tired at all. My doctor said later that I'd had the ultimate stress test.

Endeavor ended up sitting on the bottom in about sixty-five feet of water. The insurance company wanted to declare her a total loss, and most people would have just taken the money and left her alone. But her owner, Betsey Holtzmann, didn't want to give up on her, and neither did I. So we decided to salvage her.

We knew approximately where the sloop went down from the sightings I had taken. We secured the services of a diver, but he could find nothing at the marks that I had taken. He got a boat to look with a fish finder, but this didn't work so he got someone with sidescan sonar. They searched, but they couldn't find anything, either. Then another boat used sidescan sonar for two days and still found nothing.

I came home thinking that we might not ever locate *Endeavor*, but Jill Flora, who lives in Southwest Harbor and owns a Friendship with her husband, Rodney, told me about someone who could possibly help. Garry Kozak works for a company in New Hampshire called Klein Associates that makes sidescan sonars. I called him, and he agreed to come to Rockland on a Saturday and search. He arrived with two helpers and a lot of equipment: sonars, depth sounders, generators, and a global-positioning system (GPS).

We searched with the *Seven Girls* all day, towing the sonar unit over a big area. We came up empty. Finally, at about seven that night, we were about to give up when Richard suggested that we go out to where I had picked him up and tow the sonar towards the southwest. We did this and we found the *Endeavor*! We made several passes and checked with the depth sounder to make sure. Then we took an exact position with the GPS. We also dropped an anchor with a buoy to mark the spot.

Next morning, the diver went out and found the buoy drifting, with all the rope. But using the GPS, he was able to relocate the right spot and go down to check and confirm that indeed the *Endeavor* was there.

At first, we hoped that we could lift her with air bags and tow her into Rockland Harbor. The

Using Doug Beal's barge to raise Endeavor.

diver attached one bag to the bowsprit, near the bitts, and two to the traveler, on the stern. We managed to get her up so the top of the mast came out of water, but when the air bags broke the surface, the boat "bounced" and the strain pulled the traveler right out of the deck. The oak was soft from being underwater for a month, and the fasteners holding the traveler simply pulled out.

This time the *Endeavor* went down stern first. The one air bag was still attached to the bow, holding it upward as she sank, and the rudder struck bottom and was damaged. The tiller hit the coaming, cracking it and getting broken itself. Then the boom went up and struck the

spreader, breaking it and cracking the topmast. The gaff jaws were also broken.

It was obviously going to take more than air bags to lift the sloop, so I got Doug Beal to come from Southwest Harbor with his barge, put straps around her, and lift her with his derrick. In three hours the *Endeavor* was on the deck of the barge and headed back to Southwest. When we got home we found that the anchor we had dropped to mark her location was still in the cockpit. Maybe some boat had caught the line or someone had tried to pull the buoy up and parted the shackle that attached the line to the anchor.

Endeavor has since had all her original paint removed, inside and out, and she's been dried

Out of the water once again!

out and repainted. Her engine has been replaced, and the necessary repairs have been made. We put in a bronze rudderpost in place of the old wooden one, and the space under the deck in the cockpit has been sealed to create an air space. That will give her more buoyancy if she ever dips her coaming again. And we did not replace her topmast, so she'll carry a little less sail now.

All in all, it was quite an ordeal, but it's good to see the *Endeavor* sailing again.

CHAPTER *Thirty*

THE FUTURE

What I look forward to is to keep on building and designing boats and doing my history work and spending a little more time going around to different places in the *Seven Girls.*

There are still a couple of designs that I haven't had a chance to build. One is a motorboat in the old-fashioned tradition: a long, narrow, open boat with quite a bit of flare to the bow and quite a lot of camber to the stern. It would just have a spray hood on the bow, like they used to do, and I'd make it nice and fancy, with plenty of brightwork on it—real yachty looking.

The old *Leader* was like that. She was quite racy. She had a little flagpole up on the bow with the Northeast Harbor pennant on it and a big flagpole aft with a yacht ensign. Not like today, when people use little short things with little bits of flags. The *Leader*'s stern pole went up in good shape and had a good, big flag. That added quite a lot. There were other boats I can remember like that, too.

Those old launches were practical boats. You could put the hood down, and there was plenty of room so you could have chairs and things in them. They were good to go on a picnic in, and people went out in them to watch the boat races. With no cabin in the way, they could sit in those boats and see all around with no obstructions. I like that. It's still a good design for being out on the water.

Behind my shop on Clark Point Road in the twelve-foot rowboat I designed.

The boat I'd build would be thirty or thirty-one feet, or something like that, and today you could put in an engine that would really make it go. Some of the old boats that were built that way were quite fast. With such narrow proportions, they didn't have much resistance in the water—and back then they didn't have the powerful engines that we have today.

I'd also like to build an International One-Design if I could find somebody that could afford to have me build it the way I'd like to. The original Internationals have lasted a long time, and people still race them around here. They were built on a mold with steam-bent frames, and they were planked edge to edge, with no caulking.

I've done a lot of work on those old Internationals, and they're nice boats. But there are flaws in the construction, and I think I could do better. The way I'd like to build one is by laminating the frames with epoxy. That way, you wouldn't need molds to build the boat on. The only hardwood I know of that takes glue real good is mahogany, and that would do. There are a few things about the deck structure that could be improved on, too, with the modern adhesives and things that we have today. I'd double-plank the hull, and I wouldn't use any caulking either, except in the garboards. Of course, you'd have to keep the weight within the class restrictions, and that would be a challenge. It would be a nice boat to build, but it would be expensive.

Something else I look forward to is cruising around a little bit more in the *Seven Girls,* taking her to some places that I've been wanting to go. I've already been up the Penobscot River to Bangor, but I'd like to go up the Damariscotta River. I'd like to go up to Portland and farther down east, to Calais, maybe.

I also want to do more of my history work. One project I want to get done is the transcrip-

Me at the helm of the Seven Girls.

The Seven Girls *as she looks today.*

tion and editing of Gertrude Whitmore Carroll's journal. She was one of eight daughters in an early Southwest Harbor family that lived on Carroll's Hill. Their homestead is now owned by the National Park Service. One of her sisters died, and all the others became teachers. But Gertrude had epilepsy, and consequently, the family did not send her to school much. Still, she learned to read and write.

A woman in Bangor found five parts of Gertrude's journal which was kept in old account books, on the blank pages. They were in an auction and this lady bought them, but it was a while before she looked to see what she had. When she realized that it was history and was important, she got in touch with me somehow. I don't know just who referred her, but I realized what she had in a minute.

I told her that the best thing to do was give them to the Tremont Historical Society, where they could be preserved. So she did, with the stipulation that the society transcribe them and keep them. She also wanted a copy when they got done. In the meantime, we found two more of Gertrude's journals: she started the first one in 1888 as a seventeen-year-old girl, and she did the last one in 1917. She made the final entry five days before she died. There are still some books missing, although we may find them eventually.

One of the things this journal shows is how people helped each other back then. If somebody didn't have something and somebody else did,

Richard helping out at age three.

Richard clamping ribbands on Freedom.

Richard sailing aboard Freedom *in her first Friendship Sloop Regatta.*

they shared it. I don't think you notice that so much today. Maybe people have everything they need and think that everybody else does, too.

What I've been doing with Gertrude's journal is copying the words just as she wrote them, and I can remember many of the people that she talks about, so I'm adding comments about who they were and what they were doing. There'll be a lot of genealogy in the book and also a lot about events that happened around town. I've found some newspaper items that go along with Gertrude's account, too. It will be quite interesting, and eventually I want to get it published.

There's also a maritime history that I want to finish writing. It's about Mount Desert Island and the surrounding islands, and it's something I've

been working on for years. So far, I've found over three hundred and fifty vessels built on this island between 1782 and 1902. And it would surprise people how much tonnage was commanded by men from Tremont, which included Southwest Harbor in the old days.

For this project, there are records that I want to look up at the National Archives in Washington. I'm sure that I'll find more if I go down there, and I'd like to stay at it right steady until I'm satisfied that I have everything that I can get. That's the way I like to work. Going back and forth doesn't appeal to me. I don't like to leave off.

That's how it is for me with building boats. I like to start building a boat and work steady—

Edward's high-school graduation picture.

the old-time boatbuilders I can remember. That's what they did all their lives, and they wouldn't have thought of doing much else.

When I was a little kid I always had the idea that boatbuilding would last and last and last for generations. So I'm proud to see my children involved in the business that Marion and I started.

When Edward was growing up, he did his share of work in the shop. Early on, he showed an aptitude for design work. He had a plastic model of the *U.S.S. Constitution*, and he wanted to copy it and make it bigger in wood. He asked me how he could do it and I said, "Take the lines off the plastic model and expand it." He worked it out pretty much by himself and it turned out pretty good.

After he graduated from Mount Desert Island High School in 1982, he went to the University of Maine at Presque Isle. He was there for a year before transferring to the Massachusetts Institute of Technology. After three years at MIT, he earned his Bachelor of Science degree in naval architecture and marine engineering. He also did a year of graduate work there. He's now a very good designer, and he's been a great help in computerizing that part of our business, as has our daughter Nadine in keeping our books and running our office, and her husband Tim in building and maintaining boats and running the storage business. (Marjorie now works for the Jackson Laboratory, so she's close by as well.)

But sometimes I've wondered whether it was the right thing to do to steer Richard into the

every day, all night, every minute—and not have to stop until it's done. I like to be out in the shop making shavings all the time. You can't do that, of course. It's not humanly possible. But that's the way I like to do it.

I guess there'll always be wooden boats to build. I hope so, anyway. I think there will still be a few people who want a wooden boat, and they'll keep it going. Fortunately, we've had enough demand to keep *us* going. My interest is still there, and I'll keep on doing something with boats as long as I can. I don't know how long that will be, of course, but as long as something comes along for me to do, I'll do what I can.

I've always thought something like boatbuilding ought to be long-term. To make good boats you've got to stick with it year after year, like all trade. Actually, I don't know if I really steered him into it, but he took to it, and I didn't discourage him.

Even when Richard was three years old, he was out here in the shop, working. One time I was getting ready to clean the bottom of *Heironymous*. I got my boots on and had my buckets and a broom, and I was going at it. Well, I looked around and here was Richard coming with *his* bucket and *his* little broom and *his* boots on. So he's been doing something with boats for a long time, ever since he was just a little tyke. He's in it, and there's no out of it now. And Richard can put wood together better than I can.

He's like me when I was bit by the bug. After I had built one boat, I couldn't wait to get started on the next one, and it's been that way ever since.

Richard aboard Acadia *in 1998.*

Glossary

adze	Ax-like tool used for shaping timbers.
aft	Toward the rear of the boat.
Alden, John G.	Prominent twentieth-century Boston yacht designer and naval architect.
ballast	Weight added to the interior or exterior of a boat to provide stability.
boom	The horizontal spar (pole) that is attached to the mast to anchor the base (foot) of the mainsail.
bow	The forward end of the boat.
blocks	Pulleys.
bowsprit	A heavy, fixed spar (pole) that extends forward from the bow of the boat to carry an additional forward sail (jib).
Buttocks, buttock lines	In lines drawings, profiles of the hull as if it were sliced lengthwise at regular intervals outboard of the centerline.
camber	Curvature or arching (of a deck, for example).
catboat	A type of sailboat whose mast is stepped (positioned) far forward and whose sails are usually gaff-rigged.
caulking	The process of packing and sealing the seams between planks in the hull. Or, the materials used therein.
caulking iron	A flat-bladed tool used in conjunction with a mallet to drive caulking into the seams between planks in a hull or deck.
CCC	The Civilian Conservation Corps, a public-works program that provided jobs during the Great Depression of the 1930s.
centerboard	A movable keel that can be swung out of the way or lifted up to allow a sailboat to travel in shallow water.
centerboarder	A sailboat built with a centerboard.
coaming	A raised band of wood that goes around the cockpit of a boat to keep out water washing across the decks.
come about	Changing a sailboat's direction to bring the bow across the wind, which requires the crew to be alert and reset the sails on the other side of the boat.
coasting schooner	A sailing ship engaged in trading (carrying cargo) along the coast.

cuddy	A small enclosure that provides storage or protection from the elements and spray; usually located forward in the boat.
cutwater	An extension of the stem under the bowsprit, normally found in boats with a clipper bow.
deadwood	A timber or timbers that go between the keel and the shaft log.
dinner pail	A traditional metal lunch box.
double-ender	A boat that is designed with a pointed (rather than square) stern.
down east	As a direction, eastward along the coast of Maine; as a region, the area approximately east of the Bucksport bridge. I often say that "down east" is east of wherever you are at the moment.
dragger	A type of commercial fishing boat that is rigged for towing a funnel-shaped net (trawl) along the sea bottom.
gaff	A spar (pole) that is attached to the mast at one end and supports the upper edge of a sail.
garboard	The first or lowest plank in the hull, directly next to the keel.
GPS	A satellite-based global positioning system widely used in navigation.
gut	A narrow passage or waterway.
hackmatack	A larch tree.
haking	Fishing for hake.
half model	A scale model of a boat's hull as if it were split longitudinally; created by the boatbuilder or designer to visualize the desired shape. Can be used to take measurements when constructing the full-size boat.
Herreshoff, L. Francis	Famous New England yacht designer during the great age of wooden boatbuilding.
jib	Triangular forward sail.
jib sheet	The line (rope) used to trim (pull in or let out) the sail.
jointer plane	A plane with a long base, useful for squaring or beveling the edges of wooden planks.
ketch	A two-masted sailboat with the smaller mast stepped (positioned) forward of the steering station or rudder post.
knot	A measure of boat speed equal to one nautical mile per hour (1.15 statute miles or approximately 1.85 kilometers per hour).
leeward	On the side of the boat away from the wind.
lines drawings	Design drawings that define the shape of the hull in two dimensions.

lofting	The process of scaling up the lines for a boat to create full-size patterns. Traditionally accomplished with battens on a flat floor, lofting today is often done on the computer.
lobster smack	A sailboat with a wet (flooded) well, used to keep lobsters alive during transport along the coast.
make-and-break	A type of simple two-cycle engine.
molds	The cross-sectional patterns used to define the shape of a wooden boat during construction. Also, the full-size concave forms inside which a fiberglass hull or other component is laminated.
naphtha	A highly flammable, petroleum-based fuel used in some early boat engines.
one-design	A class in which all boats are of the same basic design or style.
picket boat	The type of vessel used by the Coast Guard for patrolling harbors during World War II.
plumb stem	A bow whose leading edge is approximately vertical.
port light	A boat's window.
purse seiner	A commercial fishing boat that deploys a circular net which can be drawn tight at its bottom edge to enclose a school of fish such as herring.
"Ready about. Hard alee."	Announcement to the crew that the skipper is about to push the rudder to the leeward to turn the bow of the sailboat across the wind (i.e., *come about*).
rolled down to her rails	A term used to describe a boat heeled (tilted to one side) so far that the guard rails (gunwales) are in the water.
rudder	The blade-like structure attached vertically to the stern for steering; may or may not be fully submerged.
S-boat	A one-design class of racing boat originally built by the Herreshoff Manufacturing Company in Bristol, Rhode Island.
sawing a handline	Working a fishing line back and forth in a sawing motion over the guard rail (gunwale) of a boat.
schooner	A sailboat that has two (or more) masts with the forward mast(s) usually being shorter than the other(s); traditionally gaff rigged.
sheer	The curvature or sweep of the upper edge of the hull as seen from the side.
shoal place	A shallow stretch of water.
shoal draft	Shallow draft, meaning the boat can travel in shallow water.
skeg	An extension at the after end of the keel, designed to anchor the rudder post. Or, a shallow, plank-like keel projecting straight down from the deadwood.
sloop	A single-masted sailboat whose sails are aligned fore-and-aft, rather than crosswise to the hull (as they would be in a square rigger).

spar	A pole that supports or extends a sail, such as a gaff, boom, or bowsprit.
stations	Positions along the keel at which molds are set up during the construction of a wooden hull.
steam bending	Heating wood in a steam box to make it flexible during construction. Dry wood can easily be bent into place for ribs in a hull or around a mold for a coaming in this way.
steam launch	An open pleasure boat powered by steam.
stem	The vertical timber at the bow of the boat.
stern	The rear or back part of the boat.
stove all to pieces	Broken up, as in a severe grounding.
stuffing box	The watertight fitting through which the propeller shaft passes.
tiller	The lever attached to the rudder for steering a boat.
trailboards	Decorative trim boards attached to the *cutwater*, which they may also strengthen.
transom	Informally, the stern of a boat. More specifically, the transverse timbers that are part of the stern assembly.
traveler	Attached to the stern deck of a sailboat, a metal, usually rectangular fixture that allows the tackle for the boom to shift from side to side as the boat changes direction.
trawl	A long, relatively heavy fishing line rigged with baited hooks at regular intervals and anchored at both ends. Also, a funnel-shaped net towed by a *dragger*.
trawling	The two types of commercial fishing that employ the gear described immediately above.
tunnel stern	A stern with a hollow designed to allow the propeller to be protected within the body of the hull.
waterline	The horizontal line where the boat meets the water.
waterlines	In lines drawings, profiles of the hull as if it were sliced horizontally at regular intervals above and below the designed *waterline*.
weather helm	The tendency of a sailboat to "head up," or turn into the wind by itself.
yawl	A two-masted sailboat with the smaller mast stepped aft of (behind) the steering station or rudder post.

Boats built in the "old shop" behind Ralph's grandmother's house

Launched	LOA	Type/Name	Power	Built for
1946	15'	Lapstrake dory		Ralph Stanley.
1949	14'	V-bottom outboard		Ralph Stanley and later sold.
1953	28'	Lobster boat (never named)	4-cylinder Scripps, replaced by a 6-cylinder Chrysler and later a Ford Falcon engine.	Ralph Stanley for handlining and going back and forth to Cranberry Island. Sold to Charlie Gilley.
1953	26'	Lobster-style pleasure boat (not named)	Gray Marine, rebuilt by Westerbeke.	Dick Yates. Later owned by Earl Alley. Boat eventually burned.
1955	14'	Half model for outboard	15 HP Johnson outboard.	Raleigh Stanwood.
1957	28'	Lobster boat	Chevrolet gas engine.	Oscar Krantz. After Oscar died, the boat was sold to Alan Spurling, then sold to an owner in Connecticut.
1958	28'	Lobster boat *Betty Lou*	Chevrolet gas engine.	Roland Sprague of Islesford (Little Cranberry Island) for lobstering and fishing. Built from a half model.
1958	28'	Lobster-style pleasure boat	40 HP Volkswagen engine.	Merritt Bean for a cottage on Long Island in Casco Bay.
1959	26'	Lobster-style workboat	120 HP Palmer gas engine.	Mrs. O'Brien, Seal Harbor. A new design drawn on paper. Now owned by James Rich of Tremont.
1960	33'	Lobster boat *Seven Girls*	120 HP Palmer gas engine. Now has Ford diesel.	Chester Stanley (Ralph's father). Built for fishing. Based on 32' model. Lines taken from a half model.
1961	33'	Lobster boat *Rachel Ann*	Palmer gas engine.	Emerson Spurling. Same model as Ralph's father's boat. For fishing and lobstering. Emerson Spurling starts working with Ralph.
1962	33'	Friendship sloop *Hieronymus*	Originally 22 HP Palmer gas. Later Westerbeke 45 HP diesel. Third was Universal 50 HP diesel.	Albie Neilson. Ralph's first sailboat and his first Friendship.
1963	26'	Lobster style *Skipper*	20 HP Palmer gas engine. Later 40 HP BMW diesel.	Mrs. Lincoln Godfrey of Northeast Harbor. Same model as Mrs. O'Brien's boat. Later sold to Peter Forbes and renamed *Annie T.* Marion's father worked with Ralph on this boat.
1963	28'	Lobster style	2-cylinder Detroit Diesel.	Howard Power. Same model as Roland Sprague's boat.
1964	32'	Lobster boat	120 HP Palmer engine.	Carroll Chapin of Isle au Haut. Wanted a boat with not much flare in the bow for better visibility. Built from a half model.
1965	34'	Lobster boat *Wolfhound*	Converted 292-cu.-in. Chevrolet gas engine.	Wendell Scavey. New model, designed on paper. Used trawling for hake and handlining for pollock in the summer. Later sold to an owner in South Bristol.
1966	34'	Lobster boat	Converted Chevrolet gas engine.	Russell Pettigrove. Same model as Seavey's. For lobstering. Later sold to Frankie Chalmers. Lost to fire.
1966	35'	Lobster boat *Lorilynn*	Originally had an 8-cylinder Buick engine. A Caterpillar diesel was put in during the 1980s.	Junior Bracy of Cranberry Island. Built on the same 34' model as Pettigrove's and Seavey's.

1967	33'	Lobster boat *Wandabob*	6-cylinder Chevrolet gas engine.	Shirley Phippen of Southwest Harbor. Based on the same design as Ralph's father's boat and Emerson Spurling's boat, but built with a nearly plumb stem and higher sides than Ralph's usual design.
1967	36'	Lobster boat *Willie Marie*	Chevrolet gas engine.	Elwin McCauley of Stonington. Same model as 34'/35' design, extended. Later sold to an owner in Biddeford Pool. Then owned by Dickie Beal in Southwest Harbor. Now owned by Tripp Estabrook. Boat is in Rhode Island.
1968	37'	Lobster boat *Inez Frances*	4-cylinder Caterpillar diesel.	Emery Krantz. Same model as 34-footer but lengthened, widened, and deepened. Rigged for lobstering and shrimp dragging.
1968	31'	Lobster boat *Bette S.*	Gasoline engine.	Emerson Spurling, Jr. Based on the 28' model. For lobstering. The 12th boat built with Emerson Spurling, Jr.
1969	33'	Lobster boat *Linda G.*	V-8 Palmer gas engine.	Danny Graham (Massachusetts). Same model as other 33-footers.
1970	36'	Lobster boat *Ajax*	Diesel.	Buddy Lawson. More flare in the bow than the usual design.
1971	26'	Rebuilding of the original Friendship sloop *Venture*	No power originally. Later had a Volvo 2-cylinder 20 HP diesel.	Work done at Jarvis Newman's shop in Manset. Boat had been owned by Jarvis Newman, who sold it to a Mr. Porteous of Portland, who then hired him to rebuild it.
1971	33'	Lobster boat	Chevrolet gas engine.	James Robbins of Stonington, who was himself a boatbuilder.
1972	44'	Lobster boat *Nancy & Ricky*	6-cylinder Caterpillar diesel.	E. Richard Davis of Provincetown, Mass. Mahogany planked and "built quite heavy." Last boat built in the old shop.
1973	31'	Rebuilt the original Friendship sloop *Dictator*	Westerbeke 20 HP 4-cylinder diesel.	Jarvis Newman of Southwest Harbor. Work done in Newman's shop. Became the model (plug) for Newman's fiberglass Friendship-sloop hulls.

Boats built in the new shop on Clark Point Road

1973–1974	26'	Friendship sloop *Amos Swan*	2-cylinder 25 HP Volvo diesel.	Ed Kaelber. Became a partner in the business. Eventually sold shares to Richard Stanley.
1975	29'	Rebuilt original Friendship sloop *Amity*	2-cylinder 25 HP Volvo diesel.	Rebuilt for James Russell Wiggins. Later owned by Mr. Wiggins's granddaughter Patsy. Currently being used by an owner in Belfast for sailing parties.
1975	38'	Lobster boat *Miss Julie*	V-8 Caterpillar diesel.	Robert Stevens of Massachusetts. Built for offshore lobstering with bunks in the bow. Launched in February. Current owner, Fred Dauphinee.
1976	28'	Rebuilt original Friendship sloop *Morning Star*	20 HP Westerbeke 2-cylinder diesel.	Robert Wolfe.
1976	28'	Friendship sloop *Freedom*	20 HP Westerbeke 2-cylinder diesel.	Richard Dudman.
1977	26'	Friendship sloop *Peregrine*	20 HP Westerbeke 2-cylinder diesel. Second engine 3-cylinder Yanmar diesel.	Peter Blanchard. Designed "exactly" like the *Amos Swan.*
1978-'79		Rebuilt R-class racing boat *Jack Tar*	Outboard on a bracket.	Mrs. David Rockefeller.
1978	32'	Lobster boat *Rita Ann*	Slant-six Chrysler.	Danny Chalmers. Used as model for Newman 32. Now owned by James Bracy.
1979	25'	Open-cockpit Friendship, influenced *Endeavor*	Originally no power. Mudge: 2-cylinder 20 HP Volvo diesel. Holtzmann: 3-cylinder Yanmar diesel.	Built on speculation and kept by Ralph for a time. Originally had beach rocks as movable internal stone ballast, later replaced with lead. Sold in 1981 to Shaw Mudge of Harrington, Maine. Mudge later sold to Betsey Holtzmann.

1979	36'	Passenger boat *Poor Richard*	Perkins diesel. Later V-8 Caterpillar diesel.	Rick Savage. Built on the same molds as the 38' workboat design, "just shortened up." Now owned by Fred Smith of Rockport, Maine.
1981	44'	Lobster boat	6-cylinder Caterpillar diesel.	A local fisherman.
1982	28'	Sailboat *Rose*	First, 6 HP BMW diesel. Second, 6 HP Yanmar diesel.	Peter Godfrey. based on L. Francis Herreshoff design for *Rozinante.*
1983	28'	Schooner *Equinox*	Outboard on a bracket.	Centerboard, shoal draft. Given to Mystic Seaport, sold to an owner in Westerly, Rhode Island, then bought and brought back to Southwest Harbor by Dennis Kavanaugh. Built by Ralph with help from Richard.
1983	36'	Lobster boat *Linda G*	V-8 Caterpillar diesel.	Danny Graham. Built on molds of the 38' boat for Stevens, but shortened by 2'. Powered by V-8 Caterpillar diesel. Co-built by Ralph and Richard.
1984	21'	Similar to Herreshoff Fish Class *Folly*	Sail only.	Built on speculation and later bought by Mr. and Mrs. W. Dixon Stroud. Design adapted by Ralph. Co-built by Ralph and Richard.
1985	19'	Friendship-influenced open sailboat *Bucephalus*	Sail only.	Peter Forbes. Built as a boat a boy could handle. Was the subject of Hope Wurmfeld's book *Boatbuilder*. Has a club topsail. Co-built by Ralph and Richard.
1986	19'	Friendship-influenced open sailboat *Little Folly*	Sail only.	Mr. and Mrs. Stroud. Co-built by Ralph and Richard.
1988	28'	Friendship-influenced open sailboat *Dovekie*	Sail only.	Frank Newlin. The 19' design "blown up." Co-built by Ralph and Richard.
1988	28'	Lobster-style powerboat *Nathaniel*	6-cylinder 175 HP Volvo diesel.	Morris Zukerman. Bass-boat style with a canvas top on the shelter. Mahogany used on top. "Quite fancy." Co-built by Ralph and Richard.
1989	29'	Lobster-style family boat *Peggoty*	6-cylinder 175 HP Volvo diesel.	Mr. and Mrs. Peter Harwood. Built on the same molds as the 28' model, lengthened. Co-built by Ralph and Richard.
1989	19'	Friendship-influenced open sailboat *Summer Joy*	Sail and electric motor.	Built for Steve Kleinschmidt and family. Stern post a little more plumb. Some modifications to accommodate batteries and motor. Now owned by Bob and Cindy Robertson. Co-built by Ralph and Richard.
1990	29'	Lobster-style family boat	Volvo 6-cylinder 200 HP diesel.	Mr. and Mrs. Ed Roney. Like Harwood's boat. Co-built by Ralph and Richard.
1991	30'	Lobster-style powerboat *Ruddy Turnstone*	Volvo 6-cylinder 200 HP diesel.	Peter P. Blanchard III. Built on the same molds as the 28' model, lengthened. Co-built by Ralph and Richard.
1993	36'	Lobster-style powerboat *Cinchona*	250 HP John Deere diesel.	Harry R. Neilson, Jr. Fully equipped with appliances and "a lot of brightwork." Co-built by Ralph and Richard.
1994	25'	Flat-bottom river boat *Belle*	3-cylinder Yanmar diesel.	Holyoke Whitney. Lapstrake boat, 5' wide. Owner plans to use to cruise the upper Mississippi River. Co-built by Ralph and Richard.
1995	21'	Friendship sloop *Ralph W. Stanley*	Yanmar 2-cylinder diesel.	Mrs. Franchetti. Home port is Sardinia, Italy. Has an elliptical transom. New bowsprit and second jib added in 1998. Mainly built by Richard.
1996	21'	Cutter-rigged sailboat *Resolute*	Outboard on removable bracket.	Dr. Hugh Harwood. Ralph's design based on an old English cutter: "long, narrow, deep." Gaff-rigged with a club topsail. Outside keel. Mainly built by Richard.
1997	16'	Friendship-influenced open sailboat *Timothy M.*	Sail only.	Mike Rindler. Scaled-down version of the 19-footer. "Boy's boat designed with a lot of reserve buoyancy." Mainly built by Richard.
1997	28'	Schooner *Dorothy Elizabeth*	3-cylinder Yanmar.	Roger and Mary Duncan. A new design, although similar in profile to the *Dovekie* (same under the water). Named for their mothers. Sails by Nathaniel Wilson. Duncan rigged the boat himself. Mainly built by Richard.

1998	28'	Friendship sloop *Acadia*	3-cylinder Yanmar.	A new model. Built for Adrian Edmonson. Ralph drafted her on paper. Home port is Dartmouth, England. Mainly built by Richard.
2002	44'	Lobster boat	300 HP John Deere diesel.	Chris Lutyens, Johnston, Rhode Island. Designed by Ralph and Edward. Built by Richard.
2004	36'	Friendship sloop *Tamara*	4-cylinder 50 HP Yanmar.	South Bristol, Maine. Designed by Ralph and Edward. Built by Richard.
2004	21'	Sailboat	No power.	Planked-up hull for an owner to finish. Design modified by Ralph and Edward.
Work started in 2004	36'	Pleasure lobsterboat	465 HP Yanmar diesel.	Tom Chappell, Monhegan. Designed by Edward and Ralph. Being built by Richard.

Rowboats

1977	10'	Rowboat for shop		Ralph's original flat-bottom design. (Still in use.)
1977	10'	Rowboat		Flat-bottom design built for *Peregrine*.
1981	10'	Rowboat		Flat-bottom design built for Shaw Mudge.
1991	12'	Rowboat		Dixon Stroud. Lines taken from an original Arthur Spurling rowboat.
1995	10'	Rowboat		Flat-bottom design built for Mrs. Franchetti. Ralph's design. Like boat built for the shop. Richard made one for himself.
1998	10'	Two rowboats		Flat-bottom design built for sale.
2002	12'	Rowboat		Spurling model built for Polly Saltonstall.
2003	12'	Rowboat		Spurling model built for Michael Rindler.